£5

G000149233

Presented To:

_____

From:

_____

Date:

_____

In Love, Where I Belong

In Love, Where I Belong

HOW TO EXPERIENCE GOD'S LOVE

BRENDA D. VANWINKLE

DESTINY IMAGE® PUBLISHERS, INC.
P.O. Box 310, Shippensburg, PA 17257-0310

"Speaking to the Purposes of God for This Generation and for the Generations to Come."

This book and all other Destiny Image, Revival Press, MercyPlace, Fresh Bread, Destiny Image Fiction, and Treasure House books are available at Christian bookstores and distributors worldwide.

For a U.S. bookstore nearest you, call 1-800-722-6774.
For more information on foreign distributors, call 717-532-3040.
Reach us on the Internet: www.destinyimage.com.

ISBN 13 TP: 978-0-7684-3839-0
ISBN 13 Ebook: 978-0-7684-8976-7

For Worldwide Distribution, Printed in the U.S.A.
1 2 3 4 5 6 7 8 9 10 11 / 13 12 11

Dedication

Dedicated to my husband Jim. In our more than 30 years of pursuing God's heart together, your love and kindness have been a rock I could count on. And just think: the best is yet to come! You're my knight in shining T-shirt and blue jeans—and Ephesians 6 armor. I love you.

For my dad, Edgar Paul Dixon. Now that cell phones have done away with telephone booths, I wonder where you change. I've known about the cape for a long time, Dad. (The large "S" on your T-shirt gave it away.) Thank you for living out Romans 8:28 for all to see. You're my hero.

Acknowledgments

Our children: Beth, Caleb, and Sarah, Kimberly and Ashley—my greatest cheerleaders, my greatest joy. My love for you knows no bounds.

Debbie: No dearer sister or friend has ever been found. Thank you only begins to convey my gratitude. Your heart looks remarkably like Jesus.'

My Peculiar Tribe: Anita, Dawn, Lara, Ranee, Shirley, Summer, and Wendy (and your patient husbands!)—there are no truer friends or greater prayer warriors. You are the best, and I love you.

FIRE group: Ben, Chris, and Marena, Jordan, Luke, and Summer—your special place in my heart is branded there forever. Keep burning with His passion.

Chuck, Barbara, and Trisha: Thank you for believing in me when it wasn't logical to do so. Your lives have changed mine.

Bill and Kris: you have provided a safe home to grow in and be launched from. Thank you. Who you are is turning the world upside down.

Pam: You first gave me permission and the challenge to write. Thank you.

Tim: Your kind yet persistent pressure to pursue the writing call is greatly appreciated.

Darryl and Sheila: Only eternity will tell how many lives you have changed forever.

Anna and Judith: Friends, prayer warriors, and encouragers—I'm so thankful for you.

Mike: You got the ball rolling. Thanks for the push.

Jo Robbins of AfterWord: if the Queen of England ever forgets her native tongue, I shall point her to the Editor of English Extraordinaire! Thanks.

Pastor Marv, Ray, and Dorothy: You provided quiet havens for me to begin my writing journey. This is that. I thank you.

Destiny Image: Each step of the way you have made this a blessed journey. I'm so grateful.

Endorsements

In Love, Where I Belong takes the reader on a journey of restoration. The reader is able to leave the devastation of brokenness and discover a path of healing and wholeness. Brenda VanWinkle will capture your heart as she walks you from defeat and abandonment to a life filled with God's unconditional love.

In Love, Where I Belong will cause your heart to sing again. You will dare to dream again. Allow your life to be ignited with a love that never disappoints. I recommend this book for anyone searching for fulfillment in life!

> *Barbara Wentroble*
> President, International
> Breakthrough Ministries
> Author, *Prophetic Intercession*;
> *Praying With Authority*; *Rise to Your Destiny,*
> *Woman of God*; *Removing the Veil of Deception*

In her book *In Love, Where I Belong*, Brenda VanWinkle paints a beautiful picture of the love of the Father that transcends rejection and abandonment. In this powerful manuscript Brenda teaches us the difference between the orphan spirit and the spirit of adoption. She demonstrates how each of us was individually selected by God Himself to be a member of the royal family.

This book will rescue you from the clutches of fear, break through the obstacles of offense, and heal the scars of shame. Brenda's personal story will inspire you, encourage you, and give you practical wisdom to live the abundant life that has been promised to each of us in Christ. I highly recommend this book to anyone who struggles with a sense of powerlessness or low self-esteem.

Kathy Vallotton
Senior Leader of the Bethel School of
Supernatural Ministry
Redding, California

Contents

Foreword

…we spend our years as a tale that is told

(Psalm 90:9b KVJ).

You are good [God], *and do good.*
Teach me Your statutes

(Psalm 119:68 NKJV).

Introduction

Of all our shared childhood dreams, singing like Julie Andrews and dancing like Ginger Rogers were the ones that most quickly lit a fire in our eyes. After all, my sister and I were growing up in the 1960s, a time when television was the up and coming social phenomenon.

I was about ten years old when my parents bought our first color television set. The whole family was amazed to see our favorite shows in dazzling color instead of black and white, even if faces were a bit green in those early days of Technicolor! Some shows were so much like rituals that we could set our clocks by them. We weren't about to miss an episode!

Saturday evenings at our house could mean only one thing: *The Lawrence Welk Show*. Oh, the glitz and glamour! Any show that started with an explosion of music and bubbles filling the air could only be a good thing, and week after week my family tuned in. As it was a musical entertainment and variety show, there were all sorts of talents on display. The handsome young men in their light blue leisure suits, each of their long-enough-for-the-young but not-too-long-for-the-old locks of hair perfectly in place. And the girls! Not only were they beautiful, but they were dressed in long, flowing gowns. Come to think of it, the entire cast looked like they were heading to the prom!

To my young eyes it looked like a dream. As I watched Cissy float across the stage in Bobby's arms, smiling at the camera and waltzing by as though the two of them were the happiest people on earth, it was sealed in my heart: someday, somehow, I, too, would dance and sing like that. I would. I must.

When the hour was up and the television turned off, I was always a bit shocked to find myself sitting in my pajamas with pin curls in my hair. My feet had no idea how to perform the steps that my heart had just executed flawlessly, and when I sang, my brothers still told me to shut up. What a harsh reality to realize that I was just me, and that singing and dancing were obviously not a dominant component of my DNA.

My sister Debbie and I refused to be discouraged and decided that we would wait for as long as it took. Oh, we knew we had the desire, and we also never stopped believing that one day we would dance and sing. This time around, Julie and Ginger would be in awe of us, even though we admitted that it likely wouldn't happen until we got to Heaven.

Can you relate? Can you remember a time when you just ached to pull a great move on the dance floor that would leave the crowd in awe? Did you grab a bar of soap and sing so passionately in the shower that you were a bit embarrassed to come out and face your family, knowing that they must have heard you? But at the time, the water splashing over your head and your amazing voice bouncing off the shower walls (Man, you didn't realize you sounded that good!) compelled you to sing louder, just to drown out the cheers and applause of your adoring audience. It's OK to admit it, at least to yourself. There is just something in most of us that would love to express our emotions and passion for life in such a way.

Then years go by, and we grow "too mature" for such dreams and expressions of heart. Our jobs and families consume us, and eventually even our joints tell us, "Wait for Heaven!" For some of us, the cares and burdens of life weigh down our feet, and we feel as though the only use for our voices is the effort to be heard. If any of these or other scenarios have captured your dream, I have great news for you: it's never too late!

The Bible is a love letter filled with hope and joy and promises.

The Bible is a love letter filled with hope and joy and promises. The real life stories recorded there reach across time and speak to us even today. For example, the first song and dance recorded in the Bible is performed by the most unlikely of women. The story of her debut, found in just two short verses from the Book of Exodus, is full of passion and delight. The woman's stage is a riverbank, and her "review" reads:

> *Then Miriam the prophetess, the sister of Aaron, took a timbrel in her hand; and all the women went out after her with timbrels and dancing. And Miriam responded to them, "Sing to the Lord, for He has triumphed gloriously and is highly exalted: the horse and his rider He has thrown into the sea"* (Exodus 15:20-21).

Singing and dancing—in the Bible! By an old woman! At the time, Miriam was about 92 years old. What is it that causes an old woman to grab a tambourine, gather a spontaneous dance troupe around her, and break into boisterous song? I believe it was that Miriam could no longer hold back her awe and delight in who she had just discovered God to be.

This is the same Miriam who had hidden her baby brother, Moses, in a basket in the Nile River when Pharaoh ordered the death of all Hebrew boys age two and under. This is the Miriam who had watched Pharaoh's daughter find the basket and look inside at the innocent little face that impacted her heart with the spirit of adoption. This same Miriam had grown up in slavery and watched her now adult brother Moses return from exile, confront Pharaoh, and lead her and her nation to freedom. At the time of her song and dance, Miriam had just walked through the dry bottom of a very wet Red Sea, which stood at attention to let the people of God pass through. Miriam had arrived on the other side, and as the Egyptian army pursued, she had watched the sea stand down and close in over the enemy of God's chosen people.

Miriam had heard about this Jehovah God her whole life and had even seen His power in the plagues that came to Egypt, but when she saw Him hold back the sea and save her people, something broke loose in her. Maybe the fear of being a slave washed away. Maybe the relief of finally knowing that she and her people were safe began to sink in. Or maybe she was remembering the day, 80 years before, when she had watched her baby brother saved out of another river. Whatever it was, something broke the dam of Miriam's intimidation and fear of what others would think of her, an old slave woman, and she danced and worshiped and sang. Out of her belly flowed *"rivers of living water,"* about which Jesus would talk in John's Gospel (John 7:38).

What about you? What did you dream of being or doing when you were a child? Have you done that?

It's very likely your dream wasn't the same as mine. Perhaps you dreamed of composing a beautiful aria or of discovering the cure to a disease. Maybe you envisioned a building that no one else ever thought of designing, or pictured yourself as a world-class chef, even in your own kitchen at home. Whatever your dream was, I encourage you to pull it out of your memory bank, dust it off, and consider if it is still yours to pursue. I realize I will never dance or sing as in my childhood dreams, but I will press on to know and experience God in new ways, as Miriam did. I have given myself permission to enjoy each day and live it as fully as I am able. It's part of the journey of walking with a God who is good.

 Don't wait until you get to Heaven to join the party of His amazing love!

As you read this book, my prayer is that you will be reminded of the times when God, our good Father, rescued you from the slavery of fear, the intimidation of wondering if anyone would ever care that you exist, the ache of hoping you would find someone to love you, the pain of abuse, or the self-pity and shame that may have been sitting like a backpack full of rocks on your shoulders. And if you are still struggling with any of these difficulties, I pray that by seeing God as one who is in love with you—madly in love—you will find the courage and faith to give all the bondage that comes with them to Him. Permission is granted to pursue Him fully, and to begin to dream again. As you are set free and reminded of His goodness to you over the years, may you worship Him! May you dance! May you sing! Don't wait until you get to Heaven to join the party of His amazing love! Let burdens and insecurities go, and dance as Miriam danced!

CHAPTER ONE

The Look of Love

Although I knew the Book I was reading was alive, I was a bit shocked when it spoke to me. As I read in the fifth chapter of Mark and the eighth chapter of Luke, stories I had probably read a hundred times before, this time it was as though a curtain was pulled back to give me a fresh new understanding of time past.

Although I knew the Book I was reading was alive, I was a bit shocked when it spoke to me.

I saw realities I had never seen before and heard lessons I'd missed in all those previous readings. Come and look with me at an ancient series of events that are fresh and relevant for us today. They draw us into a moment of time when people not unlike you and me saw the Son of God look at them with love.

Given the importance and weight of each Word that God breathed to create His Book, we might wonder why He chose to include these particular stories. Most people in the community wouldn't have given the two main characters much thought. They were sick and dying, and each was considered unimportant, not even worth educating.

Outside their own families, their words would have carried little, if any, weight. They were low in the pecking order of society, second-class citizens, and deemed not much more than slaves.

They were women.

Looking for Hope

They were not just any women. These two were a middle-aged woman and a young girl—one past her prime, one not yet in hers—both dispensable in their society and each long past any hope for her life to improve.

The old lady—for in ancient times she would have been such—was an outcast. We aren't told much of her story, so we don't know whether she was a mother or barren. We don't know if she had been well loved by a husband before her hemorrhaging began, if she had lived alone as a single woman, or if she had been misused at the hands of men. All we know is that for 12 years she had been bleeding and that she had spent all her money, even what she had saved for her old age, to find a cure. Doctor after doctor had prescribed this medicine or that cure and perhaps even a surgical procedure, all to no avail.

Their best advice had left her humiliated. The bleeding would not stop. "Unclean! Unclean!" was the name others gave her and the name the law required her to call out about herself if she ever chose to leave her forced solitude. The looks of disgust and rejection she received must have made her think twice about venturing into the city, and the loneliness of her fate was hard to bear. Sometimes pressing through her shame just to be out in the stream of life was worth the stares. She had no hope, no cure, and no chance for a better day or a new life.

On the day she met Jesus, I wonder if she was thinking back to the day 12 years before when it had all begun. What might have started merely as a rough month in the way of women turned out to be endless years of suffering. Some days were worse than others; the heavy days left her weak and light-headed, her strength seeping away with the years of her youth.

Hoping for Life

In another home in that same town, a day 12 years before had brought great joy to a family as their little girl was born. Oh what a delight she was! In a world where sons were preferred over daughters, this baby was received with shouts and laughter, tears of joy, and celebration. Her father, a leader in the local church, was delighted by this gift from Yahweh, and he doted on his little one as she grew—watched over her, protected her, and provided the best he had to offer. She was his pride and joy. And now here he was, this man named Jairus, pleading with Jesus for his little girl's life.

The one description we have of Jairus is that he was a ruler in the synagogue. When we meet him, he has also pressed through the large crowd surrounding Jesus to get close enough to fall at His feet and bring his request. Although Jairus was deeply rooted in the Jewish religious system, his desperation caused him to leave the familiarity of ritual and throw himself on the mercy of the one who was able to heal and restore: *"…My little daughter is dying. Please come and put your hands on her so that she will be healed and live"* (Mark 5:23).

The very next words in the passage are, *"So Jesus went with him"* (Mark 5:24). No hesitation. No questioning of Jairus' past. No request for an explanation as to why Jairus thought he deserved such special treatment. No three-point sermon to convince Jairus of the need for him to change. Just simply, *"So Jesus went with him"*—the Heavenly Father's heart displayed through the Son to a man desperately hoping for a miracle.

Just simply, *"So Jesus went with him"*—the heavenly Father's heart displayed through the Son to a man desperately hoping for a miracle.

We don't know if the little girl had suffered a long-standing disease or if perhaps a sudden fever had struck her down. What we are told is that her papa was desperate for a cure. Surely a man of Jairus' stature and wealth had checked all the medical possibilities and options, but we aren't told that. What we know is that his desperation led him to Jesus at the same place and time as the woman with the issue of blood.

Against All Odds

Both came to Jesus looking for life and hope. The woman came in fear and trembling. Overcoming intimidation, she pressed through the crowds and came up behind Him to touch His garment—to grab hold of the fringe of His identity—and just that was enough to heal her. Her actions gave voice to her faith.

The man came on behalf of his child who was dying. His words displayed His belief that if Jesus would just touch her, she would be healed. He came face-to-face with Jesus, humbly yet boldly seeking Him man-to-man.

One came in shame, one with courage. Both came desperate.

A Touch, a Look, a Word

It strikes me that not only did the woman know she was healed the instant she touched Jesus' clothing, but so did He. He wasn't content to wink at her from a distance or to ignore her in the midst of all the people crowding around Him. He wanted to see her. He wanted to look her in the eye and hear her story. The Word of God says that He asked who touched Him and looked around for her, and that when she came forward, He listened as she fell at His feet and told Him her story (see Mark 5:29-34).

How long do you think it had been since anyone had sought this woman out to speak kindly to her or to look at her with the look of love? How long since anyone had cared enough to listen—really listen—to her whole story? I'd venture to say at least 12 years. Oh how Jesus honored her! He didn't call her "Unclean." He spoke to her straight from His Father's heart and gave her a new name:

"Daughter." *Daughter.* She had a Papa. She belonged in someone's heart.

**He spoke to her straight
from His Father's heart
and gave her a new name:
"Daughter."**

The Touch of Life

And even as He was speaking words of life to the woman, Jesus overheard the news of death that had come from Jairus' home: "Your daughter is dead. Don't bother the Teacher any further" (see Mark 5:35; Luke 8:49).

Ah, the heart of Jesus is so wonderful! At the same moment that He had been welcoming a healed, restored daughter back into the fullness of life, He heard that another daughter was dead. Looking at Jairus, a heartbroken dad, He exhorted him, "Don't give fear any place in your mind: only give room to belief" (see Mark 5:36; Luke 8:50). Jairus had just witnessed a woman's healing and had heard that her sickness had begun 12 years ago. That was when his little girl had been born! Could he keep his faith intact for a miracle of blood to begin flowing again inside his 12-year-old daughter?

Jesus went to Jairus' home, and when He told the mourners that the little girl was only sleeping and not dead, they mocked and ridiculed Him. Putting them all outside, He went into her room with her parents and the disciples that were with Him, took her by the hand, and said to her, "Little Girl, get up!" (see Mark 5:41; Luke 8:53), and she arose out of death, out of her circumstance.

I Want What They Got!

So here we have two stories back-to-back in the Scriptures. In one of them, a middle-aged woman receives new life when Jesus stops a flow of blood and enables her to stand up and take her place in society. In the other, a proud ruler humbles himself at Jesus' feet, and his daughter, a little girl close to the marrying age of the day, rises up and walks into her destiny when His Word causes blood to flow through her veins. Both women were called "Daughter," and both mattered enough to Jesus that He stopped what He was doing to heal them.

 Jesus is the greatest respecter of women ever to have lived.

Jesus is the greatest respecter of women ever to have lived. His life and example elevated women to their rightful place as daughters of Father God, and He made it clear that women, like men, dwell and belong in His heart. Because He is *"the same yesterday, today, and forever..."* (Heb. 13:8 NKJV), we can trust that He is still very interested in women. He is still honoring us, looking for us, gazing at us with love, listening to our stories, and healing us from all that saps our strength and faith. He is longing to take our hands and raise us up so that we can walk in the dignity of womanhood and the delight of being well-loved daughters.

A New Beginning

When Jesus healed the woman and the little girl, He was demonstrating the heart of Father God. Everything Jesus did and said showed us what God is like. Even as Jesus was kind and good, so God is a kind and good Father.

According to Barbie Breathitt of Breath of the Spirit Ministries, Inc., in the Bible, the number 12 represents government. Not earthly government as we think of it, but divine Kingdom government. Some of the ways this is seen is in the fact that there were 12 tribes of Israel, 12 judges of Israel, and 12 original disciples. Each of these had to do with the divine order of God on the earth, heaven's domain impacting earthly systems. Jesus came to establish a new government: the government of God's Kingdom, Heaven come to earth. He healed a woman who had been bleeding for 12 years, and He raised from death a little girl who was 12 years old, showing the world what the Kingdom government was like. No more would women be outcasts or second-class citizens. No more would sin, sickness, and death have their way. In this new government, infirmities and afflictions would bow to the King whose Kingdom would be settled and established when He shed His blood, so that sons and daughters might find eternal life, starting here and now.

Over and over again in God's Word we see Him calling men and women, training them, and healing their spirits, souls, and bodies as they encountered love personified. Jesus didn't look past them; He looked at them and into them. The honor He displayed to women and men alike caused multitudes to follow Him wherever He went.

> The honor He displayed to women and men alike caused multitudes to follow Him wherever He went.

He hasn't changed. His heart is still good, His face is still gentle, and His eyes still sparkle with the delight of His love for those He came to save. I can trust a man like that. I can follow a Lord like that. I can love a Savior like that. Join me as we go on an adventure of discovering just how good He is—and how very deeply we belong in His heart.

Prayer

Dear Lord,

How desperately I need to know that You are good! I long to have You look at me with the look of love. I ache to hear You call my name, to know that You know who I am. My heart beats with the desire to belong in a love that is pure and safe.

Like the woman in the story, I want to push through whatever stands in my way to get to You. And like the little girl, sometimes I feel as though I can't help myself but need You to come to me.

I thank You that in whatever circumstance I am today, all I need to do is call out to You, and You will hear me, You will see me, and You will bring me hope and life. I want so much to know You as a Father I can trust. Please help me trust You. Help my heart heal. Help me rise up and live! I offer You my hand. Please walk with me until You have my heart and I know that I belong in Yours.

In Jesus' name I pray,

Amen.

CHAPTER TWO

Joy—Much More Fun Than Sorrow

"*D*on't laugh. You're in church!" How many times I heard that remark when I was a little girl! I didn't mean to laugh, but let's face it: lots of things strike a child as funny, and sometimes humor strikes in church! And you know what happens when you try to stifle the giggles, don't you? Yup, you end up snorting and then you're really in trouble!

Trying to Be Good

My grandfather and my Aunt Lois were the ones who stepped in to help raise my siblings and me when our mother died. Her death was unexpected, and she not only left a gaping hole of grief behind but also an adoring husband and four young children. What had been regarded as a rough pregnancy turned out to be the cancer that took her life. David, the baby she was carrying, was born prematurely and was a mere three days old when she died. Mom had been given the choice to abort him in hopes of saving her own life, but that was never an option in her mind, so dear David lived as a testimony to a mother's love and sacrifice.

 I guess I reasoned that the more perfect I was, the happier everyone around me would be.

My own young life was impacted by the trauma of missing Mom terribly and of not understanding why she was suddenly gone. In the only way I knew how, I tried to ease my own grief and not to further upset the adults around me. How? I would be as good as I possibly could be. I guess I reasoned that the more perfect I was, the happier everyone around me would be. I did not want to do anything to make anyone sad, ever again.

So when Aunt Lois "shushed" me in church, I wanted to be good. I really did. Aunt Lois was on one side of me and Dad on the other, so being good was really my only option.

Will Someone Please Explain?

The trouble was that not being allowed to giggle in church just never made sense to me, even then. My mind couldn't justify a somber countenance with what I was singing, such as "Joy to the World" and "He Lives!" Even at a young age, my heart would just soar when we sang the great hymns of faith, and it's hard to stay quiet and still when your heart is soaring.

And there was another thing I didn't understand. In Mrs. Ferguson's catechism class, I diligently memorized the short catechism as I was required to do. I wanted Mrs. Ferguson to think I was a good student, I wanted my parents to be proud of how good I was, and I wanted to work hard enough so that God might someday like me, too! But it was the very first question I had to memorize that messed me up: "What is the chief end of man?" Answer: "Man's chief end is to glorify God and enjoy

Him forever!" What? How could I enjoy God forever if I couldn't laugh in church? It just didn't add up.

How could I enjoy God forever if I couldn't laugh in church? It just didn't add up.

A Heart for God

At the tender age of four, my heart was already captured by loving God. When my older siblings went to school, I pulled out old Sunday school papers, lined my baby dolls up against the furniture, and witnessed to them about Jesus' love. I actually remember crying as I pleaded with them, "Please accept Jesus so we can be in Heaven together!"

My heart was tender, but my understanding of who God is was skewed and wrong. My concept of being His child was not so different from the requirements of Buddhism, in which one is never sure of having bowed low or frequently enough, prayed enough, burned enough incense, or offered enough fruit. Except for the details, I was like the Buddhists, trying to be good enough to get God to love me and be pleased with me. It was a hopeless cause, because I never would be good enough. I had not yet learned that it was also a waste of time because He already loved me, without condition. I did not yet know that He was already pleased with me, that He wasn't angry with me and wasn't out to get me. I really believed it was up to me to be "good enough"—but just how good was enough? I did not yet know that He was—and is—good, and it is on His goodness my longing to be loved is fulfilled.

Growing Confusion

My young mind was also grappling with another issue, which was the whole idea of the Trinity. Again, I wanted to make everyone, especially God, like me, so I worked really hard to understand how God could be three persons in one. No matter how hard I tried, I just couldn't make sense of it, so whether influenced by someone else's teaching or by my own limited reasoning, I came to a completely and totally wrong conclusion: Jesus was definitely the good guy who came to protect us from the mean and angry Father, for whom I could never do enough, and the Holy Spirit was a ghost.

I was terrified of ghosts, so it was best to leave Him be. I saw the Father as an ancient man with a long, flowing beard, leaning forward in His throne so He could keep an eye on me, but I never saw Him looking at me with love in His eyes. My perception was that He was just waiting for me to mess up, which He and I both knew would be only a matter of time. I only saw disappointment and dissatisfaction expressed on His face, and I knew it was because I just was not as good as I should be. He seemed to me like a judge in the sky with a huge flyswatter, waiting to discipline me for doing something awful, like laughing in church. Can you relate? The problem was, my concepts of God were completely opposite from what the Bible says about Him. My religion was not much more than a church version of pulling petals off a daisy and chanting, "He loves me, He loves me not." In my mind, it all depended on what kind of mood God was in that day—and how good I'd been.

I Needed Help!

What a huge, horrible lie I believed, both about God and about myself! What a huge, horrible burden for anyone to carry, especially a child! I'm so thankful that John 17:11 sets the record straight. There, Jesus tells us that He came to show us the Father and that He and the Father are one. I'm so grateful that I can rejoice over what He told the disciples: *"...Anyone who has seen Me, has seen the Father..."* (John 14:9). Jesus said that when He talked, He was just repeating what He'd heard the Father say, and that when He did something, it was because He'd seen the Father doing it. What a revelation!

It must mean that Father God is good, because what Jesus said and did brought hope and life to everyone! He healed people's bodies and their relationships. He brought justice and righteousness to the earth. He offered peace. If Jesus was the exact representation of the Father, then the Father also wants all those wonderful blessings for us (see Heb. 1:3a). Yes, I had been right about Jesus being the good guy, but once I realized that Jesus' life manifested the heart of the Father, I knew that the Father was good, too. As for Holy Spirit, John 15:26 says, *"But when the Helper [Holy Spirit] comes, whom I shall send to you from the Father, the Spirit of truth who proceeds from the Father, He will testify of Me"* (NKJV). Three good guys! I had the Trinity!

Once I realized that Jesus' life manifested the heart of the Father, I knew that the Father was good, too.

If you want to know what Father God is like, look at Jesus. If you want to know what Holy Spirit is like, look at Jesus. *"...He is altogether lovely..."* (Song of Songs 5:16 NKJV).

We can read the Bible and see God as a stern and rigid judge, or we can see Him as a loving Father, setting guidelines to keep His children safe and calling them to obey and love Him as a family. The way we read it makes all the difference.

Here's an example of what I mean. As our children entered the teenage years, of course that meant they also began driving. Any parent who has lived through it knows what an incentive these years are to become a prayer warrior on their children's behalf! Not only did they hold their own lives in the hands that held the steering wheel, but by heading out without adult supervision it was up to them to decide how they would spend their evening.

I remember telling them that what their father and I had tried to teach them about the ways of God were not so different from the lines painted on the side and middle of the highway. Although they knew the rules of the road, technically our young people held the wheel of the car and could drive down whichever side of the road they chose. No one could stop them from heading down the opposite side, but if they chose to do so, there were bound to be immediate and severe consequences to themselves and others. The lines were not painted on the road to punish them or keep them from having fun, but rather to protect them and others. The law caused boundaries to be set for safety and protection.

For purposes of discussion, we can say that is how the law of God works. He hasn't given us the Ten Commandments and guidelines for life to punish us because He's mad at us. He didn't set guidelines for life in place to restrict us from having fun or living fully. Rather, out of His love and compassion for us, He "marked out the highway," like the paint on the edge of the road, so we would know safe boundaries. The law of Love set limits so we, His children, would be safe. He, Himself, is The Way, our protector and defender and friend.

Sorting It Out

I used to think like this:

- Jesus loves me.

- The Father has to like me because Jesus twists His arm and convinces him to.

- Holy Spirit? I don't like ghosts and would just as soon leave Him alone and have Him leave me alone!

How thankful I am that God gives us opportunity to repent, which means to change the way we think! In repentance we confess our sin, make a choice to turn away from it, and then turn toward God's way of doing things. Whatever the misconceptions we have about Him, He is willing to show us the truth and help us know His love for us—if we just ask Him.

Untangling the Confusion

As part of blueDoor, a women's ministry that I lead, I give necklaces to the women who attend the initial weekend, so I'm always on the lookout for the best prices I can find. On one occasion I walked into a local department store, and my timing couldn't have been better. Just as the salesclerk picked up her price gun to mark clearance items in the jewelry department, I walked to the counter to see if I could find any good sales. When I began scooping up the necklaces as quickly as she could mark them down, I felt the need to explain. The salesgirl seemed to love the idea, and instead of putting them back on the display hooks, she began handing the necklaces to me as soon as she marked them. I gently draped them over my left arm, and then extended my fingers and hung them there, becoming rather like a display rack myself. Taking the utmost care to keep the chains in order as I garnered my collection, my excitement grew just imagining the women who would receive them.

Once the 51st and final necklace was marked down, I headed to the jewelry counter to pay for my bounty. Oh, so carefully I placed the entire collection on the glass countertop, but a moment later when the clerk reached to pick up just one, we discovered that they were a knotted mess! Chains of one twisted and wrapped themselves around pearls of another. How in the world had that happened? To this day I don't understand; I had been as careful as I could be!

In my embarrassment of having created such a mess, I was about to start pulling here and yanking there when the salesgirl said, "Here. I've done this a lot and I've learned an easier way." Then, being the pro that she was, she gently untangled the necklaces. While the center knot was still in a clump, the individual strands began to loosen and take shape as her fingers skillfully separated one from another. Like magic, the center knot began to disengage, and one by one the necklaces were freed from the confusing jumble. We then carefully wrapped each one before bagging them, so I could get home without doing further damage.

As I've given my life to knowing the Lord, He has, with my permission, healed me and put the fragmented pieces of my life back together into a wholeness that He can use. Just as the deft salesgirl unraveled the knotted necklaces one by one, my heavenly Papa is gently straightening my confused and tangled beliefs about who He is. As He lifts each lie out of my jumbled soul, He replaces it with His truth, and then the next lie is more easily dislodged. I now have the confidence to believe that my mind can truly be transformed by His Word.

My heavenly Papa is gently straightening my confused and tangled beliefs about who He is.

What are some of the lies that He is dislodging? That I must perform my way into His love. That He is angry with me and waiting for me to mess up so He can punish me. And what is the truth that He is planting in me? That He is a Father full of joy. That I can laugh and celebrate life together with Him—even in church! He is not angry with me, nor is He waiting to punish me. He loves me as I am. I don't have to try to earn His love or acceptance. This truly is amazing grace! And it's not just for me or for a few "special" people. Father God is waiting for all of us to offer Him our pain and confusion so He can replace them with His goodness and wholeness. All we need to do is ask, and like the salesclerk in my story, Holy Spirit will gently begin to untangle our pain and confusion until it comes into His beautiful order.

The God Named "Good"

For many years I thought how easy it must have been for the disciples who walked with Jesus for the three years of His earthly ministry to trust and believe in Him. After all, there He was, in person, performing miracles and saying things to the religious leaders that they longed to express but didn't dare say.

As I grew in understanding, I realized that perhaps being there as His ministry unfolded could have proven a huge challenge, even to those who loved Him most. Some of Jesus' sayings were, frankly, confusing and a bit hard to deal with and understand, at least at first glance.

For example, Doctor Luke recorded the story of a ruler who asked Jesus a question. Not just any question, but *the* question that could determine his eternal destiny: *"...Good Teacher, what must I do to inherit eternal life?"* (Luke 18:18 NKJV).

Wow! This is the question every person in ministry hopes to be asked! We stand ready to share about what Jesus has done and get the person saved! So I find myself shocked at Jesus' reply. Instead of explaining His virgin birth (complete with shepherds and angels), or a three-point sermon to prove who He is, His astounding response was: *"...Why do you call Me good? No one is good but One, that is, God"* (Luke 18:19 NKJV).

Of course Jesus was and is God, and I believe He wanted this questioner to process that. Also, Jesus, not yet having been glorified in His death, resurrection, and ascension, would not take glory for Himself but gave it to the One who deserved it—the Father. All goodness originates in the Father, because He *is* good. He doesn't just do good or act good. Goodness is the very essence of His being.

The Bible gives us many names for each person of the Trinity. Entire books have been written just to list and define and categorize the many names by which they are named in the Word of God. God is so big and complete in Himself, we can't possibly describe Him with just one name!

Think of all the names a person can have. For example, a man can be known as: his given name, man, husband, son, brother, uncle, brother-in-law, grandpa, cousin, pal, friend, lover, dad, buddy, nephew, mailman

(or the appropriate professional title), also kind, gener-
ous, moody, thoughtful, etc. The list could go on and on.
If we use this many words to define the various roles and
attributes of a mortal man (or woman), no wonder the
names by which we identify God are nearly endless!

In Luke 18:18, Jesus calls His Father "good." Exodus 33 is the record of a conversation between Moses and
God. In verse 18, Moses requested of God, *"Please, show
me Your **glory**."* In verse 19, God replied: *"I will make all
My **goodness** pass before you, and I will proclaim the **name**
of the Lord before you"* (NKJV).

Here God Himself equates His glory with His goodness. His glory is His goodness is His name. Goodness is
the attribute of His character God wanted Moses to see.
The word *attribute* can be broken down into two words:
the article a and the word tribute. When Moses went back
down the mountain from his meeting with God, the
Hebrew nation would be waiting to know—"What is He
like, Moses?" *Goodness* was the tribute God wanted to be
given. Of the myriad of names that could accurately define who this Father is, He Himself chose "Good" as the
name by which He wanted these former slaves to know
Him. After all their years of mistreatment by harsh and
unyielding slavemasters, He wanted them to know they
had a Father, and that He is good.

If you have believed that God is angry, scary, or a de-
manding taskmaster, or if you are simply ready to know
this God who is the wonderful Papa you've been looking
for, you can talk to Him about it. Prayer is just that: talking
to Papa through Jesus the Son. In the Lord's Prayer, found

in Matthew 6, Jesus invited us to pray saying "Father," or "Papa" to address God. What follows is a prayer you can use; or you can pray one of your own from your heart.

Prayer

Dear Papa God,

I admit it feels a bit strange to call You that, as I've never thought of You as a good Dad who really likes me. I admit that I have thought You are angry at me, that I have to be good and do all the right things so You will love me. I am very aware that not only can I not be good enough, but I'm tired of trying. Please forgive me for believing things I've heard or imagined about You that aren't true, and help me, starting right now, to know who You really are. I give You permission to start untangling the confusion in my mind about who You are, and replace it with Your truth.

Help me to see You looking at me with love, the pure love that You give freely and that I don't deserve. Help me to know You so well that to call You "Papa" will be the most natural thing in the world. I want to laugh and dance and sing and enjoy life with You. Show me how to celebrate being loved by You!

In Jesus' name I ask,

Amen.

Whether you have known and walked with Jesus your entire life or you are just meeting Him, think about the

three most common names by which you have known
Father God. Is it awkward to think of addressing Him as
"Papa"? Why?

I invite you to meet a friend of ours, Mrs. Wang. As
you look for ways the Lord was reaching out to her, I encourage you to see how He has been inviting you into the
dance of His grace as well.

Grandma Wang

It was more of a consistent dull ache than a sharp pain.
A pain can be located and medicated and eased; this was a
deep, deep ache that seemed to have no remedy, no over-
the-counter cure. It was a heartache, and as such was beyond what a touch or word could do.

I brought the ache back with me from my first trip to
The Mainland in February of 1992. Of course it wasn't
intentional and it wasn't even until we'd been home for
half a year that I realized that, like the parasites we'd been
warned lived in the water there, I had somehow picked up
a heartache along the way. It had wormed itself into the
very fibers of my heart, inching its way throughout my
desires and dreams, burrowing deep and making itself at
home. The worst of it was, it had infected even my blood
and my mind, changing me in ways I didn't know were
possible. I'd been bitten and bitten hard by God's heart
and love for China and her people—and was desperate to
find relief.

Where do you turn, who do you go to in order to re-
trieve the part of you that was left behind on the other side

of the world? I was sure I didn't know, but just being with a Chinese person would surely help.

With the University of Iowa in Iowa City being just 50 miles away I decided they might at least know where to direct me to find a Chinese person. I called their International Student Department and told them my predicament—I needed a Chinese friend; did they have any? To my amazement and delight yes they did, and she was standing right there. Would I like to talk with her? And so right there on the phone Ping and I became friends.

Ping was at the U to obtain her doctorate degree; her husband and son were also living in town. Would we like to come visit at their home on Saturday, say for breakfast? You bet we would! And armed with a pan of homemade cinnamon rolls we arrived at International Student Housing that October morning not knowing what to expect.

Ping met us at the door with TauTau, 'Tommy,' her son. Li, her husband, was busy at the stove making "Chinese pancakes," made with rice flour and filled with scallions and flavor. We shared our offerings with each other and started a relationship that would take us places we hadn't yet imagined. Ping, having lived in LA previously, was fluent in English; Tommy spoke some and Li struggled to just keep smiling through all the gibberish. We had a delightful morning together and left with our hearts full, the ache somewhat appeased by our promise to meet together again soon.

The journey had begun.

Learning to say "Ni Hao" (hello) in Mandarin seemed like such a big deal to us and we must have made our friends sick of hearing it as we walked around telling each other "Ni Hao" the next few times we were together. Maybe to distract us, maybe just to give us a cultural lesson, or maybe in an effort to have us learn more than one Chinese word, one Saturday soon after Ping asked us to go with her to Chinese school to pick up Tommy. In an old building near the apartments, classes were held each weekend for the children of visiting scholars so their children would learn how to write and read Chinese. Ping wanted us to see the school, to show off her American friends to her peers there, and to meet a teacher friend of hers, Mrs. Wang.

The classroom was at the bottom of a narrow stairway, and we dutifully filed down to see how it was set up and meet Tommy there. On the way back up I happened to look up into the eyes of a Chinese woman and, must admit, thought I was pretty clever when I could greet her in her own language. I thought all I said to her was "Ni Hao," and I thought that was an innocent "hello," but suddenly she and Ping were loudly conversing in Chinese, and I had a feeling I was the subject of the discussion. Brave as I am, I hustled up the stairs to join my family outside, putting a safe distance between The Lady and myself, trusting Ping to take care of whatever offense I may have given by saying my two little words the wrong way.

So when she and The Lady came out together looking for me, I figured it was time for an apology—in English. Instead came an introduction: this was Teacher Wang, the very lady Ping had wanted me to meet. Imagine—out of all the people in the building, she was the one I had spoken to. *Oh, if we'd have had any idea of how many more "little signs" the Lord was yet to send our way over the years to encourage us to keep moving forward!*

Wang was a professor from a university in China where she taught Mandarin Chinese to foreign students. In her mid-50s, she had been sent here by the Chinese government to try to find a school that would be willing to set up a women's college inside China—the first on the Mainland since the Cultural Revolution of the 1960s. But she had lots of spare time and was wondering: Would Jim and I like to take Mandarin lessons from her? She was willing to teach us for one hour each week in her home, for $5/lesson. Wow! This was more than we had hoped for! To learn the language, to hang around in a Chinese home, to acclimate to some of the culture and customs—yes, we were very interested. And the next week we began almost three years of weekly lessons with Teacher Wang. Each Saturday we would head to Iowa City to study, go out to eat, then off to Cedar Rapids, Iowa, to worship at River of Life Church. What rich, full days those were!

Teacher Wang soon became Grandma Wang to our children. She loved them and they her. Each week that they joined us she would greet them with squeals of joy and lots of hugs. She kept slippers and plastic flip-flops inside her front door for us to put on as we entered and took off our shoes. There were oranges and apples and sunflower seeds set out for snacks, and always, always, plenty of hugs and laughter and joy as she exclaimed over and over how beautiful and precious they all were.

We all learned so many things from Mrs. Wang—far more than language (which we actually didn't learn much of!). She wore glasses that were broken, held together at times by masking tape, sometimes worn in two pieces, being held to her head by the tilt of her neck. We thought she was poor: she taught us that what we have is often good enough.

She had us over, with Ping and family, for a Chinese feast one time. We were in awe over the amount of food as well as the fact that some of it sat and got cold while she cooked the rest. She didn't stress over having dishes that matched or food that was steaming. She gave us the best of what she had, and we learned that our best, when given in love, is what people really want anyway.

One night soon after we started lessons I had a dream. We were very intimidated by the language, and the first time we opened a book and she began making these strange and awkward sounds, expecting us to repeat them, I nearly burst into tears wondering what I was doing there. Mrs. Wang spoke almost no English so she was unable to explain what she meant except by sounds and pointing, and speaking in Chinese, which we understood not but two words of. It was overwhelming and I felt lost and insecure. Then I had the dream:

In it, I was walking toward Mrs. Wang's apartment— it was set up as a three-sided structure around a center courtyard with trees and grass. Mrs. Wang was on the ground floor of the two-floor building, and in my dream she was standing in the doorway watching me arrive. But I hesitated; in fact, I stopped as I began to walk across the yard. I was so unsure and so afraid I wasn't sure I could go to her.

Then suddenly Jesus was there. He was dancing about in the yard, tossing His head back in deep, living laughter as He held out His hand in invitation for me to come dance with Him there. Still I hesitated until He spoke to me, and though I don't remember the exact words I do know He was inviting me to join in His delight; to not miss the dance and the adventure that lay ahead. He was telling me not to be afraid as I was following in His steps—and it was *good*.

In 1994 I don't know if I'd ever heard the relatively new term "spiritual warfare" so I had no idea that's what we were in. All I knew was that ungodly people were taking advantage of our dear friend, and the only recourse we had to stop them was prayer.

While our love for Teacher Wang was deep and real—we even gave her Mother's Day gifts—we were surely not the best students she'd ever had or she'd have given up teaching long before. Raising four children and pastoring a church while Jim was working full-time didn't leave a lot of opportunity or energy to concentrate on language study, especially when we only met once a week. The most frustrating part was that we were unable to communicate with Mrs. Wang on the level we wanted to.

Therefore, when we arrived one week later to find a young Chinese man living in her spare room, we were full of questions and concern—not so much because he was living there as we'd learned that is quite typical Chinese behavior. However, there was something about him that didn't "feel" right and Mrs. Wang's behavior had changed. She was not as open and carefree and happy as she had been.

Somehow we managed to get the story: she had found a school that was willing to set up a women's college in China, and this young man was their representative. He was there working out the details and the following week was taking her to a convention in New York City to learn more specifics. While there she would be wined and dined at the finest New York had to offer, all expenses paid. Her only obligation was to listen to what was being offered and consider joining the college in its endeavors. The college making the offer was home to a large, international cult.

Ah! Our hearts were sick! How did this happen that Mrs. Wang had gotten herself tangled up with this mess? We wanted so much to tell her what the school was, and how concerned we were but didn't have the language to express it. However, I think she read our hearts on our faces and knew we were deeply concerned.

The young man would not let us have any time alone with her; whether it was intentional or his own curiosity about us, I don't know. Finally he went outside for a moment and when he did we expressed as best we knew that this was not a good idea and to please be very careful. She told us she didn't feel good about it but was now committed to the New York trip. Although she didn't know God and didn't understand the words we said, we prayed with her for protection and courage to do what was right. We left her home with heavy hearts that night and began a week of intense prayer and fasting for what was happening. To think of this cult getting a foothold in China through our dear Teacher was more than we could handle, and we knew we had to pray it through.

When we saw her two weeks later the young man was gone and Mrs. Wang told us she had told the school "No" to their offer. They weren't happy with her, but she sensed that to go forward with it was wrong, and in respect to our deep feelings decided it was something she could not do.

Weeks later our Teacher told us her visa would soon expire so she would be returning to China. At our farewell we met at Ping's home for a simple meal, then with their permission showed them the Jesus video in Mandarin.

When it was over Mrs. Wang told us: "I feel like I am a little lamb. There is a large circle of people holding hands and Jesus is standing in the middle of them and He's calling me to come. Come, Wang! Come!"

We prayed a simple prayer that Mrs. Wang would accept the invitation to join the circle of the redeemed, and said our good-byes. In the years since we have lost track of our dear teacher and friend, but think of her often with deep affection.

Wherever you are today, Mrs. Wang, may your dreams be fulfilled as you take hold of Jesus' hand, follow His lead, and dance.

CHAPTER THREE

How Did We Get in This Mess?

*G*enesis 1-4 tells the story of the first man and woman that God created, Adam and Eve. Created in His image and likeness, God's first family shared perfect life and perfect love in a perfect environment. In other words, they enjoyed each other's friendship and company. I can imagine Eve laughing at all of Adam's jokes and Adam listening intently as Eve shared her feelings with him. (This was paradise, remember?!) Eve wouldn't have been creeped out by mice and spiders, and Adam didn't have to lay awake at night wondering how he'd pay the bills. What a great life! Sounds like a place I'd like to live.

The story of creation, the very first story recorded in the Bible, is a story of God's goodness. In reading the account we see that after everything He created, He looked it over and saw that it was good. And when He crowned His creation on the sixth day with making man and woman in His own image, according to His likeness, He then saw that it was *very* good (see Gen. 1:31).

It took a God who *is* good to create that which is good, and to recognize goodness when He saw it.

In the beginning God created the heavens and the earth.

The earth was formless and void, and darkness was over the surface of the deep, and the Spirit of God was moving over the surface of the waters.

Then God said, "Let there be light"; and there was light.

God saw that the light was good; *and God separated the light from the darkness.*

God called the light day, and the darkness He called night. And there was evening and there was morning, one day.

Then God said, "Let there be an expanse in the midst of the waters, and let it separate the waters from the waters."

God made the expanse, and separated the waters which were below the expanse from the waters which were above the expanse; and it was so.

God called the expanse heaven. And there was evening and there was morning, a second day.

Then God said, "Let the waters below the heavens be gathered into one place, and let the dry land appear"; and it was so.

God called the dry land earth, and the gathering of the waters He called seas; **and God saw that it was good.**

Then God said, "Let the earth sprout vegetation, plants yielding seed, and fruit trees on the earth bearing fruit after their kind with seed in them"; and it was so.

The earth brought forth vegetation, plants yielding seed after their kind, and trees bearing fruit with seed in them, after their kind; and **God saw that it was good.**

There was evening and there was morning, a third day.

Then God said, "Let there be lights in the expanse of the heavens to separate the day from the night, and let them be for signs and for seasons and for days and years; and let them be for lights in the expanse of the heavens to give light on the earth"; and it was so.

God made the two great lights, the greater light to govern the day, and the lesser light to govern the night; He made the stars also.

God placed them in the expanse of the heavens to give light on the earth,

and to govern the day and the night, and to separate the light from the darkness; and **God saw that it was good.**

There was evening and there was morning, a fourth day.

Then God said, "Let the waters teem with swarms of living creatures, and let birds fly above the earth in the open expanse of the heavens."

God created the great sea monsters and every living creature that moves, with which the waters swarmed after their kind, and every winged bird after its kind; **and God saw that it was good.**

God blessed them, saying, "Be fruitful and multiply, and fill the waters in the seas, and let birds multiply on the earth."

There was evening and there was morning, a fifth day.

Then God said, "Let the earth bring forth living creatures after their kind: cattle and creeping things and beasts of the earth after their kind"; and it was so.

God made the beasts of the earth after their kind, and the cattle after their kind, and everything that creeps on the ground after its kind; and **God saw that it was good.**

Then God said, "Let Us make man in Our image, according to Our likeness; and let them rule over the fish of the sea and over the birds of the sky and over the cattle and over all the earth, and over every creeping thing that creeps on the earth."

God created man in His own image, in the image of God He created him; male and female He created them.

God blessed them; and God said to them, "Be fruitful and multiply, and fill the earth, and subdue it; and rule over the fish of the sea and over the birds of the sky and over every living thing that moves on the earth."

Then God said, "Behold, I have given you every plant yielding seed that is on the surface of all the earth, and every tree which has fruit yielding seed;

it shall be food for you; and to every beast of the earth and to every bird of the sky and to every thing that moves on the earth which has life, I have given every green plant for food"; and it was so.

God saw all that He had made, and behold, it was very good. *And there was evening and there was morning, the sixth day* (Genesis 1:1-31 NASB).

Because God created mankind as individuals with free will, He put two distinct trees in the garden. From one, the Tree of Life, Adam and Eve were welcome to eat whenever and as often as they liked. From the other, the Tree of Knowing Good and Evil, they were forbidden to eat, because while God wanted them to live forever in agape perfection with Him, He never wanted them to taste the horrors of knowing both good and evil.

Perfection was gone, and in its place came accusation, suspicion, and fear.

You know the story. Satan, their enemy (and ours), came to them, and they fell for his temptation to eat the forbidden fruit. In doing so, they chose satan's way instead of God's plan, and the Bible says that "their eyes were opened and they realized they were naked" (see Gen. 3:7). They no longer saw each other as they had before they sinned, but felt vulnerable and unsure with each other. Perfection was gone, and in its place came accusation, suspicion, and fear.

Not only did Adam and Eve begin to forget God's goodness, they began to be confused about love.

Let Me Count the Ways

One way to describe what happened between Adam and Eve is that they began to operate in a different sort of love, one that was selfish and grossly inferior to the perfect love they had previously known. Instead of looking at each other and their Father God with pure love, their eyes were opened to both good and evil. Innocence was gone, and with it their ability to think the best of each other.

In English we use one word for love, and it covers a lot of territory. We can love ice cream, love sunsets, love a television show, and love our dogs. The word is overused and therefore doesn't always carry the level of impact we want to convey when we express our love to those who are especially dear to us.

Adam and Eve lived in agape love with each other and with the Father until sin entered the picture.

The Bible's New Testament is written in the Greek language, which has numerous words for our word *love*. *Agape* is one of those words. *Agape* refers to love that is given freely, a complete love with no hidden or selfish agendas. It's what we call *perfect* love and is given even to the point of sacrifice. Adam and Eve lived in agape love with each other and with the Father until sin entered the picture. Sin distorted and ended their ability to give and receive love unconditionally. Their agape was replaced by an inferior conditional love that said, "I will if you will," or "I will as long as you do." Their perfect love for one another, as well as for God, became tainted with self-awareness and self-protection, and it became the sort of love that protects one's own interests and offers a way of escape when the going gets tough.

A Simple Example of Agape

Here's another way to think of it: I love my children with agape love as much as I am humanly able. I would do anything legal and everything within my power and means to help or bless them. When they hurt, I hurt. When they are doing well, life is happier for me. When they don't honor me, I am sad and disappointed, but it doesn't stop me from loving them with everything in me. I would lay down my life for my children, because I *agape* them.

While pie is surely the most perfect food ever created, I don't agape pie. I will love a piece of pie now and then, but eventually my self-interest will conflict with eating it, and I'll find a way to escape its enticement. I will refuse to buy pie, or if there's one around, I will do my best to ignore it. My relationship with pie is significantly less sacrificial and binding than my love for my children. There's a big, big difference between agape love and conditional love!

No wonder we become so confused about what genuine love is; what it acts and looks like! Thankfully, Holy Spirit is busy restoring to us the remembrance and understanding that our Father is good and He is love. As His Kingdom advances and Heaven comes to earth, what our first parents lost in The Garden is being restored to us.

Back to The Garden

Remember how well Adam and Eve started out in The Garden? Their willful disobedience was not a complex plot on their part, but rather the simple act of eating a piece of fruit that God had clearly and specifically told them not to eat. The Bible says that when they ate it:

> *Then the eyes of both of them were opened and they realized they were naked, so they sewed fig leaves together and made coverings for themselves* (Genesis 3:7).

Innocence was lost as their eyes were opened to see evil for the first time. One of the first effects of sin we see in this passage is their effort to cover it up so God wouldn't notice. Unfortunately for them, they grabbed fig leaves to make clothing for themselves. I wonder how long it took them to realize that leaves shrink when they dry. I suspect they were still more naked than they realized as the day wore on and the fig leaves dried out!

The word translated as "naked" in this passage comes from a root word that means "to be (or make) bare...to make cunning (usually in a bad sense)...beware, take crafty [counsel]...."[1] So now our naked first parents began looking for a way of escape from their shame and from the mess they had made. I suspect Adam's jokes suddenly didn't strike Eve as all that funny and can imagine Adam tuning Eve out as she verbally processed what had just gone wrong. We are certain that they started a blame game that is still played today; we see it demonstrated when Adam says to God, *"The woman You put here with me—she gave me some fruit from the tree, and I ate it!"* (Gen. 3:12). Whoa, Adam! No more "laying down my life for my woman" (agape), but rather an attitude of "I'm outta here! This relationship isn't working so well for me anymore." That was not the sort of love that Adam knew before sin came into his life.

Agape the Person to the Rescue

Thankfully, God always has an answer for our sin problem because God *is* agape love, and agape love is complete. It doesn't lack any good thing but is filled with compassion, patience, peace, joy, hope, encouragement, kindness…the list is endless. In sending His agape to us in the person of Jesus, the Father gave us a way to deal with the selfish and incomplete love that we inherited from Adam and Eve. By believing that Jesus is the Son of God and accepting His payment for our sin when He died on the cross, we can receive a fresh new start at living in agape love. When we do, it changes everything.

God *is* agape love, and agape love is complete.

John wrote:

*For God so loved the world that He gave His only
begotten Son, that whoever believes in Him should not
perish but have everlasting life* (John 3:16 NKJV).

Our Father God, Agape Himself, gave Jesus out of
agape. *Freely* gave. No selfish or hidden agenda on His part.
Had He given Jesus out of selfish love, what I feared as a
child would have been true: we would have been required to
work hard enough and be good enough to gain everlasting
life. But the Father *is agape* and can only give what He has,
so He gave us His Son from His heart of agape—no hook in
this love, no need for proof that we are worthy of it. Just pure
and perfect love given freely. Wow, that's really good news!

How Agape Handles Brokenness

Interestingly, the Greek word translated as "perish" in
John 3:16 means "to destroy fully...perish...die, lose...."[2]
This means that Father God "agaped" Jesus to us so that
we would not be totally destroyed, but would live fully here
and now as well as in eternity. Acts 3:21 tells us, *"...heaven
must receive* [Jesus] *until the times of restoration of all things,
which God has spoken..."* (NKJV). Father wants to restore
agape love to us and to enjoy with us the perfect agape relationship that He enjoyed with Adam and Eve before the
Fall. He wants that for you and me; He wants us freely able
to love and be loved by our Father, Daddy, Papa God.

The same word *perish* appears in the story of the feeding of the 5,000 in John 6:1-14. Jesus had just crossed
the Sea of Galilee and upon landing, had sat down on the

mountainside with His disciples. A crowd had started gathering, and Jesus knew that the people, about 5,000 men, would need to eat soon. A little boy donated the five small loaves of bread and two small fish he had packed in his lunchbox, and as Jesus blessed and then distributed the bread and fish to those who had come, the food multiplied. All 5,000 people ate their fill of fish sandwiches, and the disciples gathered up the leftovers, which filled 12 baskets. The Bible quotes Jesus saying to His disciples, *"...Gather the pieces that are left over. Let nothing be wasted"* (John 6:12). The word *wasted* here is the same Greek word translated as "perish" in John 3:16, which means destroy fully, perish, lose, or die.

 I find it significant that Jesus didn't want to waste even the leftovers.

I find it significant that Jesus didn't want to waste even the leftovers. The story doesn't tell us what He did with them, but due to the care He took to be sure they were collected, I am confident that they weren't thrown out but were used later for someone's dinner or breakfast. My point is this: if Jesus was thoughtful and tender enough not to want broken pieces of bread to go to waste, how much more concerned is He that the broken pieces of our lives be gathered up and restored? No matter what any of us have been through, the Father's heart as expressed through Jesus is to pick us up, put us back together in wholeness, and use our lives to nourish other people with the life we have received from Him.

Jesus Loves Even Me

I've had a lot of broken pieces in my life. How about you? If you have too, I encourage you to take a moment right now and talk to Jesus. Ask Him to show you what broken pieces of your life He has picked up and made whole, and thank Him for that. Then ask Him to show you what broken pieces remain, and ask Him to gather those up in His agape and make something beautiful out of them. Tell Him you don't want any of your experiences, however joyful or hard, to be wasted. Thank Him that as He puts you back together in His love, you will have hope and peace and love and courage with which to feed other people.

Remember that old saying, "Sticks and stones may break my bones but words will never hurt me"? That was one stupid saying! Personally, I never did have a stick or stone break one of my bones, but have had many instances where words hurt me deeply.

How would you describe your heart as a child? Did every little thing bring pain to your sensitive soul, or were you like Teflon and everything seemed to "run off your back" without sticking? Or were you somewhere in between?

Ask the Father to show you how believing a lie (or perhaps many lies) shaped how you think; how you view yourself and others; how your ability to trust others was impacted.

Consider this: What if the painful things said and done to and about you are not true? Suppose—just suppose—that the Daddy who created you never once thought those bad and negative things about you? That you didn't deserve the treatment and wounds you received? What would that mean for your life now, today?

The following story tells of a time in my life when it seemed that all I had were broken pieces. It was when I first believed the lie that I didn't have a voice: that what I had to say was not important and no one would want to listen, anyway. Going through it was horrible, but it is an example that we'll look at again later to see how God can redeem even the worst of events and use them for good if we will let Him.

The Fowler's Snare

I don't remember asking for this much. I'm not complaining, mind you. Rather, I'm amazed, and I often wonder how I, of all people, have come this far in my journey. There were road signs along the path of my life, signs I dared to follow so that I could see and experience where they might lead. It's true that I didn't foresee the road being so rocky and full of turns, but I also didn't anticipate the joy of a journey walked well.

I was six years old, and I was showing off my skipping ability for my Grandpap. He was duly impressed but challenged me with, "But can you skip backward?"

With a little effort and practice, I found that I could, and I discovered that sometimes skipping backward gives one a whole new perspective…

Seemingly without reason, every Monday found me feverish and ill.

What my family remembers most about the year I was eight is that I always woke up sick on Monday mornings. Seemingly without reason, every Monday found me feverish and ill. On the days I was allowed to stay home, all it took was the bus driving away from our house to bring about a sudden and complete cure. No one knew what to make of this, and I was not able to tell them.

Mrs. Fowler, the third grade teacher at Coal Run School, didn't like me. It wasn't just the usual, "Mom, the teacher doesn't like me and that's why I'm getting bad grades" kind of dislike. My grades were high, and I wouldn't have dared tell my stepmom what was going on. I had enough trouble without adding her accusations to my life.

Every Friday afternoon, Mrs. Fowler came to my desk and whispered a random word to me, and this word became my passkey to enter her classroom on the following Monday morning. If I didn't remember the word—and I don't recall ever remembering it over the weekend—I was consigned to stand in the hall while my classmates hung their coats in the coatroom, put their sack lunches on the shelf, and lined up their tablets and pencils on their desktops. Standing in that institution-green hallway, listening to them start their Pledge of Allegiance, my mind spun, full of words, as I hoped it would land like some good-luck top on the magic word that would grant me favor and access.

Once all my classmates were settled, Mrs. Fowler would come to me in the hallway and once again ask for the long-lost prize. When I couldn't give her the word, she would point at me and let me know just how little respect she had for my heritage and home. That was on the good days. I've often wondered if she herself remembered the word that she had whispered spitefully on Friday.

I always assumed that the weekend hadn't gone well for Mrs. Fowler on the Mondays that she waited until after she had explained a math equation on the blackboard before bringing me into the classroom. Knowing that math was my weakest subject, she paraded me to the board in front of all the class and demanded that I work the figures chalked there. Whether because of ignorance or sheer terror, all the numbers looked the same to me, and none of them added up. At this point, Mrs. Fowler would turn me to face the class and tell my coal-miner family classmates, "If you ever want to know what stupid looks like, this is it. You're looking at what people call a 'stupid farmer.'" I'm sure that she said more, but somehow I never heard much but my own choked sobs. Amazingly, I don't remember the other kids ever laughing at me or calling me names then, at recess or any other time; nor do I remember ever crying in front of Mrs. Fowler. That was one victory I withheld from her.

The truth is that Mrs. Fowler really *didn't* like me. Or maybe what I should say is that Mrs. Fowler hated the Jesus within me.

Putting Vickie and me together was her mistake. In the three rows of two side-by-side desks, she put the two of us at the back by the windows. Who cared what she was talking about up there? Vickie and I had the whole world outside our window and imaginations big enough to fill the sky that we kept our heads in! Imaginary friends and fantasies and other worlds came and went through our hearts, and we whispered and giggled as fast as the clouds scuttled over the hills of western Pennsylvania's coal valley.

Even better than our imagined friends were the ones we kept hidden in our desks, safely tucked away from Mrs. Fowler's stagnant heart. These were friends bought with a price each week, ransomed with my quarter allowance from the plastic wrap that held them fast on Murphy's Five and Dime shelf. For a quarter I could buy two little plastic erasers dressed to look like Chinese people, and what Mrs. Fowler didn't know was that Vickie and I were never really in her classroom. We were in any number of Chinese villages, talking in a strange language that only we and our secret friends understood, loving and being loved in return.

**Mrs. Fowler didn't know
that Vickie and I were
never really in her classroom.**

I knew words that Mrs. Fowler knew nothing about.

He who dwells in the shelter of the Most High will abide in the shadow of the Almighty.

I will say to the Lord, "My refuge and my fortress, my God, in whom I trust."

For He will deliver you from the snare of the fowler and from the deadly pestilence.

He will cover you with His pinions, and under His wings you will find refuge; His faithfulness is a shield and buckler.

You will not fear the terror of the night, nor the arrow that flies by day,

nor the pestilence that stalks in the darkness, nor the destruction that wastes at noonday.

A thousand may fall at your side, ten thousand at your right hand, but it will not come near you.

You will only look with your eyes and see the recompense of the wicked.

Because you have made the Lord your dwelling place—the Most High, who is my refuge—no evil shall be allowed to befall you, no plague come near your tent.

For He will command His angels concerning you to guard you in all your ways.

On their hands they will bear you up, lest you strike your foot against a stone.

You will tread on the lion and the adder; the young lion and the serpent you will trample underfoot.

"Because He holds fast to Me in love, I will deliver him; I will protect him, because he knows My name.

When he calls to Me, I will answer him; I will be with him in trouble; I will rescue him and honor him.

With long life I will satisfy him and show him My salvation" (Psalm 91:1-16 ESV).

ENDNOTES

1. Strong's Concordance, s.v. "'aram," OT 6191.

2. Strong's Concordance, s.v. "apollumi," NT 622.

CHAPTER FOUR

A Time of Restoration

*N*ot only is the Lord restoring individual lives, but He is restoring His Church as well. As His children are being awakened to the reality of His intense love for them as individuals, a passion for His presence is impacting and changing us corporately. Little by little, day to day, as we walk with Jesus, it's as though we're slowly but surely being healed and made strong to know our heavenly Father. More and more we are able to hear the invitation He has given to be part of His family, to be whole.

A Sure and Steady Recovery

It wasn't the crowded sidewalks that caused us to stare. Having visited China frequently in the 1990s, my husband Jim and I had adapted well to the masses of people everywhere we went. We had seen many things that were strange to us and thought we'd become pretty well accustomed to the unexpected, but the first time we saw an intravenous (IV) stand rolling down the sidewalk with the patient still attached to the drip line, we were shocked!

In this remote part of China, penicillin was considered the wonder drug in those days. We heard about people of all ages going to the doctor with all sorts of ailments, all receiving this miracle drug through drip IV. It seemed that regardless of whether the medical issue was as minor as a cut or headache or much more serious and even life threatening, the prescribed cure was the same: drip IV penicillin.

The Chinese people have always loved fresh air and exercise, so to them a little thing like being attached to an IV was no reason to stay indoors! The sidewalks became dotted with patients carrying IV needles in their hands, shuffling along to the squeaking, scraping wheels of their metal walking companions that faithfully held the healing fluid at the needed height. And as the crowded press of humanity hurried to various destinations, the pace on the sidewalk would slow, and the crowds would make way for the one being healed. Time and space and a slow, steady drip of penicillin were given to restore health and hope to the one who was connected to the source of healing fluid.

**Little by little… I have
realized that I am connected
to my heavenly Father's
love at all times.**

There on the sidewalks of China, I witnessed a pattern I could apply to my own life. Little by little, sometimes in the most unlikely ways, I have realized that I am connected to my heavenly Father's love at all times. Though I've so often been unaware of it, looking back I can see that as I've stayed in relationship with Him, the truth of who He is and His love for me has been like those IVs, dripping truth and life and hope into my mind and soul. His Word and His presence heal me as I walk through time and space each day, staying connected to the source of life.

Drip, drip, drip.

The Process of Healing

The IV penicillin story is also a simple word picture of the Holy Spirit's work in the world today. As we look at how we, as His people, have come to our present understanding of His ways, we see the effects of the healing, restoring flow of His presence in the present-day Church.

The word *reform* means to form again, so reformation is the state of being formed again. Just as Papa God reforms us to be more like Him as we give Him our brokenness and ask Him to heal us, He has also re-formed His Body, the Church, over the centuries.

The early Church was born at Pentecost, when the Holy Spirit was poured out (see Acts 2). No drip method here! Until approximately A.D. 325, the Church was known for salvations, the power of God, signs, wonders, and miracles. Christians were known for their love of one another, and they were very relational as they met in homes to celebrate their faith in Christ.

The Dark Ages began in the mid 300s when the Emperor Constantine took control of the Church. He "became a Christian," he established Christianity as the official religion of his empire, and he set the rules. This began a thousand years of dark, difficult days for the known Western world as the Church weakened and lost much of her power. The Church needed to be healed.

Then, in the early 1500s, what has become known as the First Reformation came to the Church through a monk named Martin Luther. As he read the Bible, Luther's understanding was re-formed; he recovered the revelation that salvation is not through the works that we do, but by grace through faith. He rediscovered that salvation is a gift from God that we receive by accepting the finished work of Jesus on the cross. So the first re-forming of the Church had Jesus as its emphasis. Jesus was invited back to church.

Drip, drip, drip.

People were again dreaming of recapturing what the early Church experienced as normal.

The 1850s to the 1990s brought about the Second Reformation. This time the Church was reformed through healing revivals and the breaking out of Pentecostal and Charismatic movements. There was renewed energy and activity in the Church as God restored much of what had been lost. People were again dreaming of recapturing what the early Church experienced as normal. This re-forming of the Church was centered on Holy Spirit. Wow! That same Holy Ghost I'd feared as a child I now understood as being kind and good and wonderful to know. Holy Spirit was now welcome in Church.

Drip, drip, drip.

Many of you reading this book were living during the Second Reformation, whether you knew it was happening or not! In this revival, the emphasis in the Church looked something like this:

- You needed to believe and to make a decision for Christ.

- You had to change in order to fit in. No more drinking, smoking, dancing, or whatever your particular church believed was wrong. Unfortunately, there wasn't much practical help given for achieving the change you wanted. And it was frustrating, because you knew that until you changed enough, you would never belong.

And isn't that the goal? Doesn't everyone long to belong somewhere? And if you can't even fit in the Church, maybe this religion thing doesn't work for someone like you. Or me. Or anyone.

That was the hopeless religious world so many of us grew up in.

An Agape Revelation!

However, the Third Reformation is going on right now, and you can get in on it! In fact, you are wanted, and you belong in it.

From the 1990s to the present, an Agape Reformation has been going strong! It is characterized by a fresh discovery of the heart and love of Father God, of His outlandish love for us, so freely given with no hidden agenda. We're living in a time of wonderful opportunity, as the Spirit of God is giving us a new depth and understanding of who He is and how very much He loves us. Yes, He is a God of justice and is holy. Yes, we are to be in awe of Him as we see how hugely magnificent and pure and glorious He is. But in this day and hour, He Himself has turned the spotlight on the fact that He is our Father and He is good. In the midst of a fatherless generation, He is inviting us home.

Extreme Home Makeover

"Wow! You must really love this guy to be willing to live here!" My stepmother's shocked exclamation was in response to her first sight of the house where Jim and I planned to live after our marriage in 1980. Neither of us could blame her. The old farmhouse, whose original rooms were built in the 1860s, wasn't exactly ready for a home and garden magazine. Sagging porches, overgrown weeds in the lawn, creaking floors and a kitchen from another era were only the beginning of the work that needed done. The old house had seen better days.

Where others saw an old, dilapidated building we were able to see our dream house. We were young and in love and tore into the old house with great joy and gusto. Old plaster out; drywall in. Ancient plumbing and cupboards replaced, new windows and furnace installed. And soon, what had been a run-down eyesore was transformed into a lovely, inviting home where we raised our four children. There was laughter in the walls of our farmhouse palace as we loved and lived and grew up there together. Friends came in droves from all over the nations to spend an evening or a week, feeling the comfort and peace resident in our home. You see, restoration changes everything.

Seeing Him As He Is

As surely as we restored our old house, Holy Spirit is restoring the Church. In place of seeing Heaven as a safety net to be scared into ("Get right with God so you don't go to hell!" is surely a motivation based in fear!), we are realizing the invitation we've been given to experience agape.

Papa God is replacing our old, religious mindsets of who He is with the knowledge that we belong in His heart. His presence is the home we've been longing for. The renovation of our first love is helping us remember whose we are.

Love Starts in Heaven

Agape is the Greek word for complete, perfect, unconditional love. One of the ways that agape is expressed is written in First John 4:19, which says *"We love Him [God] because He first loved us"* (NKJV). I could not love God if He hadn't loved me first, because I can't give away what I don't have.

One of my favorite examples of this is a story of Peter and John, two of Jesus' disciples, found in Acts 3:1-10. The story took place after Jesus had been resurrected and gone to Heaven. Peter and John had gone to the temple for prayer in the middle of the afternoon. The gate they went through to enter the temple was named Beautiful. In front of this gate sat a cripple, a man who had been lame his whole life due to a birth defect. Every day a friend or family member would carry him to the temple and lay him in front of the Beautiful Gate so that he could beg. On this particular day, he called out to Peter and John as he saw them going into the temple, hoping to get some money from them. He had no idea what he was about to get instead!

Peter and John looked directly into the man's face and commanded him, *"…Look at us!"* (Acts 3:4 NKJV). The crippled beggar looked up at them, lifting his right hand, expecting a few coins to be dropped in. It must have shocked him when Peter, looking into his eyes with the look of love, said:

> I don't have any money to give you. But what I do have is faith in the name of Jesus Christ to heal and restore, so I'll give you that! In Jesus' name, stand up and walk! (See Acts 3:6.)

Peter took the beggar by his extended right hand and lifted him up off the ground where he lay, and immediately the man's feet and ankle bones became strong and whole. The shocked and delighted man, who had never walked a day in his life, stood on his own two feet, walked, jumped, and leaped his way into the temple with Peter and John!

Now, all the people who regularly came to the temple recognized this man and knew he was the crippled man who sat at the gate and begged day after day. They were shocked and amazed when they saw him walking and praising God, wondering what had happened to him. And as the healed man held onto his new friends, Peter and John, a crowd gathered, amazed and eager to find out what had just gone on.

Agape: Still Loving and Healing Today

What a story! Just as Jesus could only give what He had received from the Father, so Peter and John could only give what they had received from Jesus. As Jesus was able to look with love into the eyes of a woman crippled with the stigma of hemorrhaging and then heal her, these men who had walked with Him and known Him well were able to look with love into the eyes of a crippled beggar and give Him the healing touch of Agape. Where for years people walking by had seen a dilapidated shell of a man, Peter and John saw him fully restored. The time they had spent with Jesus changed the way they saw everything. By spending time with God and getting to know Him, we, too, learn to love Him and love what He loves.

As we learn who God really is, not who we have imagined Him to be, our minds are transformed...

This is what the Agape Reformation looks like—the Kingdom of God coming to earth through the one part of creation made out of earth: ordinary people. As we learn who God really is, not who we have imagined Him to be, our minds are transformed, and we begin to believe that the world around us can be healed and restored. We realize that we don't have to beg God to meet with us; He sent Jesus because He first loved and reached out to us. Our spirits are being awakened to the reality that He longs for us to give away the agape love that He has given us, so that the Church can be reformed into the beautiful, life-giving Bride she was designed to be.

A Place Where We Belong!

In the midst of this awakening, we are starting to understand that in agape our pathway looks like this:

- I *belong* in God's heart! Because I know I belong, my faith is activated in me so that

- I *believe* He is good and has adopted me as His own! As I believe, my mind is transformed and my spirit is built up, and

- I *become* all He created and designed me to be!

You belong in Papa God's heart! Agape love does not depend on the character and nature of the one who receives it, but of the one who gives it. You can't earn His love, but you can receive it. His hand is reaching out to you. Let Him lift you out of the mindset or circumstance that has you down, and walk, leap, and dance your way to freedom.

Drip, drip, drip.

Prayer

Papa God,

I thank You that I am alive in this most exciting time in history. Thank You that You have poured out Your pure, agape love on me, even when all I expected from You was a token of Your care. Thank You for reforming my mind and teaching me how to see You as You really are. Thank You that You will never give up on me, but will always look at me with love, will always invite me to run and dance and rejoice in Your goodness. Thank You that I belong in Your heart. It feels good to finally be safe at home there.

I love you, Papa.

In Jesus' name,

Amen.

CHAPTER FIVE

I Love How You Love Me!

*S*o far we've looked at how our feelings of being un-loved and orphaned first got a foothold, as we remembered Adam and Eve's fall and its consequences for us. A hop, skip, and jump through the basics of Church history gave us a glimpse at the reason we've never felt as though we could be good enough to fit into God's family. And finally, we glanced at what the Holy Spirit is up to in our day. He is, in part, bringing back both the understanding that we belong in God's heart and the knowledge that our identity and courage come from this sense of belonging.

In this chapter, we are going to look at the concept of intimacy, to see what it has to do with our relationship with God. Webster's Dictionary defines *intimate* as "belonging to or characterizing one's deepest nature; marked by very close association, contact, or familiarity; marked by a warm friendship developing through long association."[1] Intimacy with God is knowing who He is and who we are because of Him. We'll be talking about having such a close relationship with Papa God through Jesus Christ that we, like Abraham, can be called friends of God.

Intimacy with God is knowing who He is and who we are because of Him.

St. Augustine, a Latin church father at the turn of the fifth century, is quoted as saying that there is a God-shaped hole in men's hearts and that we are restless until we find our rest in Him. I have shared with you that from a very young age I was aware of God and loved Him as much as I could, but I haven't always looked to Papa God for my identity, nor have I always turned to Him for the fulfillment of my emotional needs. Like everyone else, I have tried to fill the hole in my heart with things that aren't shaped like God. The following story is a confession of one of my earliest remembered attempts.

The Problem With Kisses

I had never stolen kisses before, nor had any been stolen from me; I think no one would have dared try. To this day, I'm not sure I actually stole them. They were freely offered. So what's the big deal? I'd already enjoyed more kisses than I deserved.

The problem with these kisses was that I had neither the desire nor the willpower to quit. Kiss after kiss—I lost control of my senses. All I knew was that there were more available and I wanted them all. I knew there were strings attached, and let's face it: someone had to pay. But none of that mattered, as the kisses fed a deep, unmet longing in my young soul. Even when I'd gone far enough that my stomach began to ache with the reality of what I was doing, self-control was gone, and stopping was no longer an option!

I was ten years old, and it was Christmas Eve. The candlelight service at church had ended, and our family of seven was at Jim and Lillian Kelly's home to celebrate the day. Before me on the table sat a sight I'd never seen at home—bowl after bowl of brightly wrapped Hershey's Kisses. Chocolate seemed to run in my family's veins, and before the evening was over, I'd had the equivalent of a full transfusion. No one ever stopped me, and I was unable to stop myself. I gorged on piece after piece, barely getting the foil wrap off one before popping another in my mouth. Joy came to my little girl's heart that night as I fully embraced a world where the kisses never seemed to end!

Looking for Love

Oh, how painfully true that story is! Even though I grew up in a wonderful Christian family, was part of the church, and truly loved God at a very early age, something was missing in my soul. How I longed to have someone tell me that I was amazing—and mean it. I didn't want to be told that what I could *do* was amazing, but that just *being me* was enough. My insides were crying out to be assured that no matter whether I did or didn't do the things I should, I would still be loved completely and absolutely and forever. Please don't misunderstand. I knew that I was well-loved in my family, but somehow that knowledge still didn't seem to be enough to fill the ache in my orphan heart. I longed to hear words over and over again that affirmed my identity and value, and in the lack of hearing those things and knowing them to be true in my heart, I tried to fill the gap with chocolate.

 How I longed to have someone tell me that I was amazing—and mean it.

Can anyone relate? I know you can, even if chocolate is not your filler of choice. Perhaps for you it has been sleeping too much or watching television without limit. Maybe for some of you it has been falling into like and then into bed with the wrong person—time after time. Or alcohol. Or obsessive exercise and the need to be the perfect size and shape. Or being the most successful businessperson in your town, with the newest and greatest electronic toys to prove your significance. There are a thousand things we could name to fill in the blank, and we all know what I mean, because we've all been there. There's nothing inherently wrong with being the best we can be, but I'm not talking about that. I'm referring to the use of those fillers to dull our pain or to fill our yearning to belong.

Seeing Into Me

Thank God there's hope! Not one of us needs to stay trapped in the cycle of pain, apathy, or compulsion. The Bible offers us keys to freedom, and in both this chapter and the next, we are going to look at two of those keys. The first one is intimacy with Papa God.

Whoa! Isn't that language a bit risqué? Isn't intimacy something to be shared between a husband and wife? Yes it is, but it is much more than that. I've heard a popular definition of intimacy as "into me see." I like that.

God looking into my heart, me looking into His.

We've already determined that Jesus and the Father are one. Throughout Scripture, Jesus is described as a

Bridegroom and the Church as His Bride. Jesus is coming back for a Bride with whom He is madly in love, for one He's already laid down His life to serve. Revelation 19:7 tells us that the Bride is making herself ready. If you have accepted the invitation to be part of God's family by accepting Jesus, by confessing Him as Lord, and by believing that God raised Him from the dead, you are part of that Bride, and as every bride knows, there's a lot of preparation before the wedding day comes! (See Romans 10:9.)

Knowing that the Father is good takes the fear out of into-me-see.

Grace for the Race

Studies suggest that the most important years in the development of a child's perspective of life are between ages one and five, and then again in the teenage years. What kinds of things can cause us to be afraid of God and not to trust Him?

Think back on your childhood. Are your memories sweet and delightful or painful and full of shame and hurt? Remember: none of us had perfect parents, and none of us will ever be perfect parents. I've heard Chip Judd, pastor of Victory Christian Fellowship in Georgetown, South Carolina, say, "I have come to believe, over years of working with and counseling thousands of hurting people, that the bottom line is this: we're all doing the best we can with what we have."

Know that you were not alone if you had a mother or father who was not a perfect role model of Father God's love. They couldn't be! Release them from any unrealistic expectations of "they should have known better." Forgiveness is the key to walking in intimacy. Give your parents, your teachers, your pastors, and whoever hurt you a gift they may not deserve—your forgiveness. It's the gift Papa God offered you through Jesus when you didn't deserve it. Now that you have been forgiven, you are able to forgive. Like Peter and John with the blind man, you can now give what you have.

Think for a moment: what is it you wish your parents had said to you? Take that longing to hear affirmation, and speak to your children what you yourself longed to hear. Go ahead—tell someone how loved and awesome they really are!

**Forgiveness is the key
to walking in intimacy.**

In an earlier chapter, we talked about how we view the Word of God. Will the lens we use find a harsh, angry judge or a good, loving father? What we see will make all the difference in how we view God as Father. The same is true when we look back over our lives. Viewing those who hurt us through the lens of, "They hurt me and I'll never trust them again!" cuts off relationship. Looking at them through the lens of mercy not only enables us to release them from expectations that they could not fill but also frees us from the burden of holding the pain.

The Look

In school, I did well in the classroom but not on the playground. Gym class was particularly painful. I was always picked last for a team, and I even felt sorry for the team captain who had to take me! I wasn't good enough at singing, either. I remember when our entire fourth grade class was going to join the fourth grade class from another town to perform a concert. The schools in our towns had merged, and this would be our first time to meet fellow students with whom we would eventually attend junior and senior high. Not only that, but the concert was to be held at the junior high auditorium, which had a balcony! Whoa! This was the big time, and we were excited, practicing singing "Inchworm, inchworm, measuring the marigolds…" in perfect timing, day after day.

Then one fateful day, it was decided that we would learn parts so that we wouldn't all be singing melody. When it was my turn to sing, my crippling shyness grabbed hold of my throat, and I could barely squeak out a note! It was so embarrassing, but I was certain the teacher knew I could really sing when I was just one voice in the many.

To this day, I remember my humiliation on the day when parts were handed out. The teacher came up to me and said, "Brenda, you won't be singing with the class." And sure enough, on the night of the concert, it was Kerm and I sitting in the balcony, listening to our classmates perform on the stage below.

But in class, I was at the top! Mrs. Cunningham always passed out our papers from the previous day, starting with the highest grade and ending with the lowest, and day after day, she would proudly look at me and say, "Well, I guess we know who is first, don't we, class? Brenda, come get your paper!" At least there was something I could do well and be applauded for.

Then the fateful day came when I heard her say, "Well, class. We've had a bit of an upset here today. Carol, come get your paper first, please." Oh no! What happened? How could I have not been the best? And when I walked up next to get my paper, Mrs. Cunningham gave me *The Look*. You know the look I mean. The look that says, "I'm disappointed in you. You didn't do your best. What's wrong with you?" The look we get when we don't live up to what is expected of us. The look given to bring condemnation and intimidation in hopes that we'll line up and behave properly.

The Look of Love

Let me assure you—that is *not* the look Papa God gives us when we come to Him! Even if we've messed up and not done our best, we are met with the look of love when we come to Him. It's the look that says, "I still love you. Let's work on this together, shall we?" Or, "I forgive you. I know you can live up to who you really are." It is just as He looked at the woman with the issue of blood and healed her and just as He looked at Jairus and saw a father desperate for his little girl to live and was moved by compassion. It is that same look of love with which He watches your life.

Even if we've messed up and not done our best, we are met with the look of love when we come to Him.

Psalm 34:15 says, *"The eyes of the Lord are on the righteous, and His ears are open to their cry"* (NKJV). *Not* with the look of disappointment, but with the look of love. Listen to how Jeremiah put it in chapter 24:6:

> *For I [God] will set My eyes on them for good, and I will bring them back to this land; I will build them up and not tear them down, and I will plant them and not pluck them up* (NKJV).

His eyes are watching us with the look of love, for our good and not for evil. As we begin to understand the magnitude of this incomprehensibly great God looking at us with love, our relationship with Him becomes more authentic. We long to spend time with Him, getting to know Him and letting Him into our dreams, because we know we can trust a love so deep and pure.

Spending time with God—sharing our hearts and learning His ways—is how intimacy with Him develops, belonging in His heart, being adored with His look of love. Who needs chocolate?

Prayer

Dear Papa,

I come to You in Jesus' name. How I thank You that You are enough for me! Lord, I forgive each person who has ever given me a look or said something to me that caused me to doubt Your love for me. I forgive each one who has embarrassed me or caused me to feel shame, and I ask You to bless them with knowing Your love.

I ask You to forgive me for all the times I have tried to fill the emptiness in my life with something or someone other than You. I repent of the times I have given someone else a look or a word that caused them to think less of themselves than You do. Please cleanse my heart and soul from all my wrong ways of thinking about myself, others, and You.

Thank You for letting me know how You care for me. It's good to feel safe and wanted and whole.

Amen.

Endnote

1. Merriam-Webster's Collegiate Dictionary, 11th ed., s.v. "intimate."

CHAPTER SIX

The Orphan Heart

hat an incredible reality, that we belong in God's heart! This great, good Father who loves us completely wants us to be His children! Even more than any good parent, He wants us to trust Him, to be willing to receive correction from Him, and to enjoy spending time with Him. He longs for us to express to those around us the amazing love and sense of belonging we have received from Him. This is simply astounding!

It Sounds Too Good to Be True

Whether due to our sin nature or to living so long with a wrong understanding of God's character, most of us find it hard to accept that we belong in His heart. After a lifetime of longing to belong somewhere, it just seems too Pollyanna to believe that God's love for us is this encompassing.

After a lifetime of longing to belong somewhere, it just seems too Pollyanna to believe that God's love for us is this encompassing.

When we find ourselves doubting the very news we have waited to hear, it sometimes stems from our having an "orphan heart." The term has become common in many church circles, but what does it actually mean? Is an orphan heart somehow different from the heart of a child who has parents?

Not being a psychologist, I can't answer that question from a professional standpoint, but as used here, "orphan heart" refers to the internal condition of people who feel that no one loves them just as they are and there is no one with whom they are completely safe.

In a perfect world, each of us would be raised in a home with parents who not only want us but blessed the day they found out we were going to be born! We would have parents who celebrate not only our birth but also who we are as individuals and the potential that we hold, and who speak life and blessing and hope to us, who encourage us as we grow, and who keep us safe and help us find our way. We would have parents who love us unconditionally, and in whose presence we are never afraid.

Of course that is not a possible scenario, no matter how hard we try to make it one.

I longed to be a mom and delighted in my children, but I fell far short of the mom I thought I would be. Even while doing the best they could, all the parents I know have said and done things they regret, things they never imagined themselves saying or doing before they became parents. Watching and judging how others parent their children is very different from actually doing the job!

Not all of us have been parents, but we've all been the children of imperfect parents. In the day-to-day reality of growing up, a longing for unconditional love, which cannot be fulfilled by earthly parents, can leave an unmet need in our souls. That unmet need is the basis of an orphan heart, therefore an orphan heart is not only found in those who didn't have both parents or who grew up in an orphanage. It also exists as a longing inside that says, "You'll never be good enough." It's the guilt that tells you when something goes wrong that you are to blame, that everyone else will be chosen for the team or group but you. Sometimes an orphan heart is expressed by the feeling that you need to take charge of your own pain, hiding and dealing with it in whatever way you can find. Or that horrible urgency that you must grab the food while it's in front of you, before someone else gets your share, because you can never believe that there will really be enough for you. It's that ache in your heart to be a little kid again, to find the biggest and safest dad in the universe and to climb into his lap and just be rocked and held. It's that *longing to belong*.

Learning From Peter Pan, the Orphan

We're all orphans, looking for a daddy. That's why the Word of God speaks so much about the spirit of adoption and about being adopted into the family of God.

We're all orphans, looking for a daddy.

As our children were growing up, one of our family's favorite movies was *Hook*. It's the story of the grown-up Peter Pan, but this suave, successful, power-driven lawyer doesn't remember that he is Peter Pan. That is, until Captain Hook comes from Neverland and steals Peter's children, taking them back to Neverland with him and issuing Peter the challenge to come get them.

On a Christmas visit to Granny Wendy in England, Peter is speaking at the dedication of a hospital wing being built in Wendy's honor. This Wendy is the grown-up Wendy from Neverland who saved lost (orphaned) boys.

In his dedication speech, Peter tells the crowd that he realizes they don't have much in common, being not only from different countries but also different backgrounds and occupations. But when he begins to give honor to Wendy, mentioning how she took him in from the cold, found him a home, and loved him, the audience spontaneously rises in a silent standing ovation. It's a powerful testimony to their love and honor for Wendy, and Peter responds with a profound statement when he says in a near whisper, "I guess we do have something in common. We're orphans."

The Common Cry

I have come to this conclusion: we're all orphans looking for our Daddy. Oh, we've been quite creative in the ways we've disguised our pain and longing, but at our core is a child's vulnerable heart, aching for a father who is totally safe and good and true, whose love will not—indeed cannot—fail us. We're all looking for Father God.

Even within those of us who know God and have personally experienced His touch, this orphan heart can cause us to live as though we don't belong to anyone. Because of our fears and ungodly beliefs, our pain and insecurities, we just can't believe that God would want us. It's as though we say to ourselves, "If I let Him or anyone else know who I really am, I'll never be adopted. I'll never find a home in Abba's heart."

The Bible's Answer to Our Cry

And yet the Bible tells us that He is our Helper, our Friend, our Defender, our Shield, our Bridegroom, our Father, our Brother, our Husband. He is all these, and He is so much more. He *is* Love. He is the very thing we long for.

 He *is* Love. He is the very thing we long for.

In His Book, God very clearly expresses His feelings about our longing to belong. He knows very well each heart's resident ache to find that place of safety and acceptance. He knows that we don't want to feel orphaned in our minds and emotions.

You may have read the Scriptures below many times before, or they may be new to you. Either way, please don't skip over them, but read them thoughtfully, putting your name in them as though they were written in a letter to you from God Himself. For in truth, they were.

> *...You can tell for sure that you are now fully adopted as His own children because God sent the Spirit of His Son into our lives crying out, "Papa! Father!"* (Galatians 4:6 MSG)

> *...Doesn't that privilege of intimate conversation with God make it plain that you* [your name] *are not a slave, but a child? And if you* [your name] *are a child, you're* [your name] *also an heir, with complete access to the inheritance* (Galatians 4:7 MSG).

There it is! The declaration from God's Word, the promise and fulfillment of the adoption papers with your name on it, signed by the Father in Jesus' blood. As His child, you now have legal access to the lavish inheritance He gives!

From all eternity Jesus is the Son of God. You and I become His sons and daughters through adoption. In Luke 2 we read that when Jesus was twelve years old He was in the temple in Jerusalem, listening to and asking questions of the teachers. When His very concerned parents found Him after three days of looking, His response to them was: *"Why did you seek Me? Did you not know that I must be about My Father's business?"* (Luke 2:49 NKJV).

Jesus gave testimony at this young age that He knew God was His Father. He was able to speak and act with the confidence that comes from knowing He was a well-loved son of a good Father.

What for Jesus was a state of being is for us a process of becoming. As we just read in Galatians 4, it is Holy Spirit who gives testimony to our spirits that we are adopted children of God. As the Spirit of God testifies we cry out "Papa! Father!" to the Dad who wanted us, and adopted us into His family.

Jesus gives us this promise: *"I will not leave you* [your name] *as orphans; I will come to you"* (John 14:18 NASB). What an incredible reality, that we will never be left alone! He promised never to leave us, so He sent His Holy Spirit to walk this life with us. And one day, He will come back for me and for you.

I Belong!

This is good news! You've been adopted into God's family! You are wanted. You are safe in God's heart. He isn't angry with you or looking for a way to discipline you. There are no foster children in the Body of Christ. If you have received Jesus as Savior and Lord, you have been adopted by the Father. He won't change His mind about wanting you. If you come through the only Door there is—Jesus Christ—the paperwork won't get lost and there won't be a legal technicality that messes it all up. God hasn't taken you on a trial basis. You are His daughter, His son. His love for you is desperate, and He'll never let you go.

 You've been adopted into God's family! You are wanted.

He So Loves the World

I am writing this just weeks after the earthquake that rocked Haiti in January of 2010, taking the lives of

hundreds of thousands and leaving thousands more orphaned. This week alone, hundreds of children have been
brought to the United States to be adopted by families full
of love, families who are waiting for a child to call their
own, to care for, and to raise with all the love they have to
give. These little ones are scared. They've just witnessed
unspeakable horror, and they are now living in another
country, seeing faces they don't recognize, and hearing a
language that is not their native tongue.

What hope can there possibly be for children who
have experienced this depth of trauma and pain? The hope
of adoption and of knowing a mother's heart that brings
comfort and a father's heart that brings security and identity to their shattered lives. And where does this amazing,
inexplicable ability to love a child that is not one's own
come from? From Father God, the one whose very name
is Love, the one who promised in the verses we just read
that He will never leave us as orphans, the one who longs
for us to know Him as our Daddy. His love chases fear
away. The spirit of adoption. Knowing God as our Papa,
our Daddy, our Refuge—that is the remedy to fear.

Prayer

Use this prayer or your own words to express your
gratefulness to God:

> *I belong to You, God! After all these years of want-
> ing to belong somewhere, it is so wonderful to know
> I have belonged in Your heart all along.*

At times I've tried to follow You closely and at times I've chosen to follow You from a distance, unsure if it was safe to get close to You. Now that I'm beginning to know You as my good Father—my Heavenly Papa—I realize that I can come to You freely and without fear. Now I know that You will always have time for me. You have adopted me into Your family, and I'm safe there.

As I learn to love You as my Father, I thank You for taking away my fear. My honor and appreciation for how holy and wonderful You are have never been greater, as I learn in a new way how much You truly love me. It isn't just words anymore: now it's becoming a reality in my soul: You love me, and I belong in You.

Papa, I love You, too.

For Jesus' sake,

Amen.

Do we know in our hearts that which could never have been discovered naturally but only communicated through the work of the Holy Spirit? Do you know the royal seal of the Prince of Princes? The seal of the High King of Heaven upon his heart? The revelation—the witness—that we are the adopted children of God.

Jonathan Edwards

CHAPTER SEVEN

Released From the Snare

*I*n our heads we can know that God loves us and has adopted us, but if we don't know in our hearts that He is with us, we still feel alone.

Doing the Best I Could With What I Had

"No! You don't mean that! Tell God you didn't mean it, Debbie!" I actually remember feeling panic wash over me at my sister's foolish and brazen declaration and knew I had to step in before God heard it and took her seriously! The two of us were walking through the fields that surrounded our childhood home, dreaming of the day that our Prince Charmings would come and sweep us off our feet. In the way of young girls' dreams, we were discussing just what each of our princes would be like.

She said the words that caused my heart to stop beating for a moment or two when she announced, "I would like to marry a pastor and be a pastor's wife!" No! Not that! Even at such a young age, everything in me recoiled at the pain and loneliness that I was sure such a destiny would bring, so even though I was the younger sister, I tried to reason with her.

Some 20 years later, I found myself wishing I could become invisible and disappear. Day after day for over a year, I had lain on the floor and wept before God, crying out to know what I had done and what I could change to make the pain of my circumstances stop. I was a pastor's wife, and everything that could go wrong was going wrong relationally. The very anguish from which I had tried to steer my sister had become my own, and it was slowly killing my identity, my courage, my destiny.

How I thank the Lord that He doesn't judge us and punish us for being on a learning curve!

Now, looking back at the season when Jim and I started living out our ministry call, I realize how many mistakes I made in my youthful immaturity and zeal for the Lord. At the time, though, all I knew was that I was repenting for everything I could think of, and my adversaries, who had just months before been my friends, were not in a forgiving mood. How I thank the Lord that He doesn't judge us and punish us for being on a learning curve! Before Him I was doing the best I knew how, but inside, my soul was torn to shreds by the turmoil of wondering what I had done that was so wrong. More important, why did it seem that I, myself, was wrong?

Perhaps God had made one mistake after all, and I was it. Over and over, with my heart aching to belong somewhere—*anywhere*—I cried out for Him to show me that He still loved me and was still with me. In Matthew 28:20 He promised the disciples that He would always be with them, but was He still with me? After all, I was sure I didn't deserve Him.

When Jesus Rewound the Tape in My Mind

Remember the Mrs. Fowler story? Where had He been then? If I was His child and in His heart, why hadn't He helped a defenseless little girl? I asked Him these questions many times during this difficult year, as I once again felt alone and desperate for His help. Then one day He shocked me with His answer. Not only was I shocked to get an answer, but I was also overwhelmed by how He gave it to me.

One day I sat quietly in His presence, and with a broken heart, once again asked Him why He'd left me alone during that year so long ago. Then, what I can best describe as a movie clip began to play in my mind. I saw myself standing in the hallway of Coal Run Elementary School listening to the class prepare for the day as my mind raced with words. I heard Mrs. Fowler coming, and there she was, standing in front of me as I hung my head in shame that I didn't deserve and wasn't mine. I looked up as she began yelling at me, and suddenly it was as though the film paused and time stood still.

 There, standing between me and my teacher, was Jesus!

There, standing between me and my teacher, was Jesus! He was smiling at me with the kindest, warmest, most understanding smile I've ever seen. He put His large hands over my ears and bent over to look into my eyes with such joy and love; then the film started and time began again. I could see Mrs. Fowler in my peripheral vision, pointing and yelling at me, but I couldn't hear her because Jesus' hands were over my ears, blocking out the lies. And I couldn't look into her face, not because my head was hung in shame, but because I was busy—busy staring into Jesus' warm gaze, into the look of love that was healing my mind and soul.

The scene then changed, and there I stood, in front of that infernal blackboard. Mrs. Fowler turned me to face the class, pointed her finger, and began her litany of my many faults. Again, there He was! Dressed in the long, white robe that I'd learned to picture Him in from Sunday school posters, Jesus stood beside me, and once again time stood still. I watched in awe as He stepped over me, totally enclosing me in the safety of that robe. I was hidden in Christ Jesus.

As the tape I was watching began to roll and my teacher began speaking accusations and lies too hurtful for any child to bear, I saw each word that she spoke in anger and hatred fly from her mouth and hit Jesus! Not one word ever touched me, because none of them got to me! *He* took each blow, and I watched my Protector God being bruised by each word. Isaiah 53:5 says:

> *But He* [Jesus] *was wounded for our transgressions,*
> *He was bruised for our iniquities; the chastisement*
> *of our peace was upon Him and by His stripes we*
> *are healed* (NKJV).

As I watched Him take the brunt of the words intended for me, I realized that although a bruise comes from an impact on the surface, it heals from the inside out. That's what was happening to me. As I saw that He was not only with me but *for* me, my heart began to heal—from the inside out.

As I saw that He was not only with me but *for* me, my heart began to heal— from the inside out.

Then, when my teacher pointed and said, "This is what a dumb farmer looks like!" I realized that she didn't mean me. In my vision, she couldn't even *see* me, because I was hidden in Christ. She was pointing at *Him* and calling Him that name. At that moment, as I saw how loved and safe I had been all along, my deeply traumatized soul began to heal. Mrs. Fowler's words had become an ugly ulcer in me, and I reopened that raw place each time I agreed with the lie that I was stupid or that I was alone. That open wound, caused by trauma, was like a hole dug for a garden. Seeds of fear, self-hatred, and bitterness had been planted in it again and again, and over the course of many years, they had begun to grow.

Oh, what a Precious Friend who would allow me, as a grown woman, a wife, and a mother, to see that He had been there with me during the darkest of times and was with me still! Knowing that I belong in His heart—really knowing it—began the process of uprooting all that wrong thinking, all those lies, all that bitterness and fear and pain so that my soul could heal. What a gift. What a Father.

He Was There in Your Painful Times

No matter what your story is or what your trauma has been, I invite you today to believe, maybe for the first time, that you are accepted by the Father because of what Jesus has already done. You don't have to do anything but accept His offer of love and forgiveness. Believe that He loves you, that He is good. Believe that He is by your side to defend and protect and comfort you, even when you don't "feel" Him. That's called *faith.*

You didn't perform or earn your way into God's view of you, and you can't perform or earn your way out. His love for you will always be the same, no matter where you've been, what you've done, or what you do. The standard is not you—it is Jesus.

**The standard is not
you—it is Jesus.**

Right now, will you take a few moments and spend them with Jesus? He's as close as your breath and is longing to heal those broken, wounded places in you. He has already borne the brunt of the bruises in your heart and mind. Right now is a good time to give Him permission to pull out the weeds of bitterness, fear, and regret, to begin dealing with the lies you've believed about yourself and others, and to begin your transformation into that beloved child you have longed to be.

Ask Him to show you how He was with you during the traumatic times of your life. Wait on Him, and expect Him to show you. His response may or may not come in the form of a video as it did for me, and that's OK. Maybe you'll be reminded of a Bible verse or a song. You might hear Him say something to you in your mind, or you may simply feel loved and warm and safe. His love for you is personal, so His way of showing you His love will be personal, as well.

Mei's Story

Jim and I were in Asia, doing a training session for pastors. At a sacrifice of time and finances to themselves, church leaders had come from long distances to receive training and prayer from us. We and our faithful team of prayer partners back home and in other nations had been praying hard about these training meetings, realizing the importance and impact our time together would have when these pastors, full of faith and courage, returned to their towns and villages. The leaders in attendance had also prayed long and hard for a peaceful, uninterrupted time of learning and strengthening.

Mei invited herself to the training sessions, so it was hard to figure why she left in a huff during each one. During every meeting, she came into the room and sat with her back to all of us on a platform behind the group. Then, when we started worshiping or teaching, she would throw something against the wall and slam the door behind her as she left. Yet within ten minutes, she always came back in, walked back up on the ledge and once again gave us her back. What in the world was up with this young lady named Mei, and how should we handle this?

Rebekkah, the leader who had called the house church pastors together for training, apologized and explained that she had not invited Mei to sit in on the sessions. She also told us that Mei's pastor had sent her to Rebekkah from her home church in the north after she had come back from two years in England, "acting crazy." No one knew what to do for her. After four months in Rebekkah's care, Mei had not changed. Outside the meetings, she would not speak or look at anyone but Rebekkah, which created real tension in the otherwise happy, loving atmosphere.

I didn't sleep much that night; I couldn't stop praying for Mei. Whatever her problem was, I knew that Jesus could set her free and longed to do it. Jim and I had no idea what was really going on, and although Mei spoke English well, it was clear that she was not about to share whatever was in her tortured mind.

Whatever her problem was, I knew that Jesus could set her free and longed to do it.

The next day was miserable. Mei's attitude only deteriorated until the time of ministry, when it fell apart altogether. Jim and I had been sharing on spiritual adoption and the Father's good heart. We had emphasized that we are adopted sons and daughters of God and that we belong in His heart, and we used many of the stories and Scriptures in this chapter. When our time of teaching ended and we invited the leaders to join us in prayer, Mei left in a fury, taking time to tell me off as she departed. We discovered then just how good her English really was!

With that, the rest of the pastors also began praying in earnest for Mei. By the end of the day, spirits of anger and rejection had broken inside her, and she repented, tears streaming down her face. A humble, gentle Mei quietly rejoined the gathering, and although she wasn't yet able to talk about what had happened, she was able to worship freely with great joy. We watched her as she was transformed in front of our eyes, from a woman filled with anger and rage to one full of peace and joy. The metamorphosis was startling, and though we didn't understand what God had done, we all rejoiced to see her happy and in her right mind.

The next morning she sought me out to tell me her story. "When I got saved, I was very happy. I read in John chapter one that we are children of God, and I believed it and was so glad. Then satan lied to me and told me I am not really one of God's children—I am just adopted and don't belong like everyone else. So when I came together with other Christians, I couldn't worship or pray. I didn't feel safe and felt like I was different from them. I felt I didn't have a right to accept His love, even though He loved me. That was why I was always being so cross with Him and His other children. Now, I realize how stupid I was!

Actually we are all adopted, and when you taught that yesterday from God's Word, I let go of the lie, and my mind and heart and emotions were set free.

"Also, before I came here I had a terrible argument with my dad and said to him, 'At least I have a good heavenly Father!' He slapped my face, but really he slapped my heart, and I decided I would never forgive him. Today when you held me in a hug, I forgave my dad. Now I am really free and I know I am God's child."

The Journey to Freedom

As we can see from Mei's story, many things can keep us from knowing that we belong in our Father's heart. While in England, Mei had been invited to a church that turned out to be a cult. She only went once or twice before she realized that the church was not right, but it was enough time for a door in her heart to open and for her to accept the lie that she alone was an "adopted" child of God and not one of His own. When she arrived back home, this internal conflict over her position in her heavenly Father's heart spilled over into conflict with her earthly dad. What a victory for her to hear and believe the Word of God, which says that we are all adopted and that not one of us is left as an orphan!

Many things can keep us from knowing that we belong in our Father's heart.

Mei has since gone home and reconciled her broken relationships, and she is reunited with her family and home church. She is growing by leaps and bounds, helping a local church leader teach others that they, too, belong in God's heart.

It's the power of belonging and the power of adoption. Thank You, Lord!

Jesus Is Our Role Model

I've heard it said that comparison is the root of all inferiority, so if you compare yourself to someone, first remember who you are. You are a child of God who has said yes to the gift of salvation in Jesus, which means that when God looks at you, all He sees is Jesus. You are *in* Christ Jesus—safe, protected, loved, secure. Jesus is our standard.

Taking Care of You

The way you learn to love yourself is by learning to let God love you. First John 4:19 says, *"We love because He first loved us."* Once you experience a touch of His love, you are then able to be good to yourself. Take good care of you! Remember that He is looking out for your good.

My husband and I often travel on airplanes, and before every takeoff, we are told that, should the cabin pressure change, oxygen masks will fall from the overhead compartments for our use. Each time that "first put the oxygen mask on yourself, breathe normally, then help anyone traveling with you" is reiterated, what remains unsaid is that if you *don't* put it on yourself first, you will pass out and become entirely incapable of helping anyone else!

To me, knowing that I am Abba's child and that He is pleased with me is like the comfort of knowing about those oxygen masks. Oftentimes in my life, when a trial or temptation comes along, I feel as though "the cabin pressure just changed." At that point the only sensible response is to cry out for God's mercy to fall on me from above. Then the Holy Spirit comes as a gentle, fresh breeze of His presence. I breathe deeply of His love, and once again I know that I am safe. From that position of being in His Presence, I am equipped and able to help those around me.

The Holy Spirit comes as a gentle, fresh breeze of His presence.

No matter what is taking place in your life right now or how the cabin pressure of your life has changed, Jesus is with you. He won't leave you as an orphan, no matter how shaky your life becomes. Take time right now wherever you are and breathe deeply of His presence and of His care for you.

Prayer

Dear Lord,

You know all that I've been through. You are aware of who has hurt me, who has misunderstood me, and what has caused me fear. I ask You to forgive me for believing the lie that You were not around when hard things happened in my life. Now that I am beginning to understand that You are good, I am also realizing that I don't have to carry my pain and unforgiveness as a barrier to keep myself safe.

So Father, in Jesus' name I ask that You take away my anger and inner turbulence and that You replace them with the reality of Your love. Help me to breathe in deeply Your healing Spirit, so that my heart beats with the rhythm of Heaven, which is righteousness, peace, and joy. I wait on You, Lord, and trust You.

I am drawn to Your love, dear Papa. To know that I'll never again have to search for my safe place—the place where I belong—causes me to know that You are my deepest friend.

With a full and grateful heart,

Amen.

Though I Ride Through the Valley

I'm so grateful when the Lord allows me to see so clearly how close and present He is to me! While He has graciously shown me His nearness on more than one occasion, most of the time my walk with Him is one of faith—trusting and believing He is with me and able to save me out of my present dilemma. The journey to Jing Hong was just such a faith adventure…

Sometimes not having "extra" money is really frustrating. On the other hand, adventures often come by taking "the road less traveled." That might be the best way to describe our first trip to XiShaungBanNa, a region in Southern China, when we journeyed there as a family on the infamous Chinese sleeper bus.

It didn't sound all that bad. A bus with beds. Passengers lay down and slept while the bus traveled through the night, arriving at the planned destination—in this case, JingHong city—the next morning. Of course it was not as efficient as air travel, but much cheaper for a family of 6. Airline tickets after all were running $125/person round-trip back in the mid-1990s when we were there; the sleeper bus was only around $30. Whoever first coined the phrase "You get what you pay for" may have just gotten off the bus ahead of us.

We had no idea where we were going or what to expect, just that a lot of folk had said BanNa was a great place inside China to visit. It sure seemed better than staying on a virtually empty campus during Chinese New Year as students and faculty would be leaving for their homes and shops everywhere would close for days, even weeks, during that time of national celebration. One of my students, our "adopted son" Ben had arranged with his friend to get us a good rate on a hotel in JingHong city, so—why not? What was one more adventure in a year full of them?

I don't really remember boarding the bus in the departure city: I think upon first sight of the conditions of it my senses shut down. What I do recall is seeing the vomit along the outside of the bus where former occupants had stuck their heads out the window and relieved the pressure from within. Hmm. Well, OK, come on kids—it can't be that bad!

I'm not sure if the sour smell of feet or the reality of the sleeping situation hit us first as we stepped on board. Imagine the shock of realization that the "beds" were narrow, hard benches along the sides and down the middle of the bus, bunk bed style. We found our "seats" and were relieved that at least we were on the bottom, as the folk previously occupying the top bunks seemed to have been the ones who got sickest. Short and narrow bunks designed for smaller bodies than ours became our first major challenge, but we managed to fit into our ark, two-by-two. It was arranged so that the person's feet on the bunk behind you were right at your head, and I remember our children declaring that because of the sour smell they might never again be able to eat anything pickled as long as they live.

Thankfully, one of my motivational gifts is that of encouragement, yet still it took everything in me to convince both myself and the children that we could do this thing. We were just getting settled and somewhat believing it could be livable (living through it seemed much more vital than having "fun," at this point) when the dead came on board. At least we think the man was dead. He was carried, stiff as a board, face-down, unmoving and unaware, by four friends (pallbearers?), each one in charge of either an arm or a leg. They processed to the back of the bus where they settled in for the duration. The dead man never got out to eat or go to the toilet or anything else, so to this day we really don't know if he was dead or alive.

The bus started out on the most frustrating journey I had taken to that point in my life. We would drive a few hours then stop for a few hours, for no apparent reason. It was nearly impossible to get a bathroom stop, and when we did it was no McDonald's. It was at a typical public toilet in rural China: a hole in the ground behind a short brick wall, men on one side, women on the other. No real privacy, no water (hence no flushing), and breathing was not advised.

Our one stop to eat was at a "bus stop" somewhere in the hinterlands. Since we couldn't identify most of what was offered we opted to fast. The veggies and meats sitting in the stainless steel bowls had been there how long? It just didn't seem worth the risk, especially considering the toilets available. Thankfully we had taken fruit and crackers along with us. Ritz crackers and Oreo cookies— two of the only western foods available to us at that time in this part of China—looked like the finest delicacies at that moment. We dined on them with perhaps the greatest prayer of thanks we had ever prayed over packaged food. With Ritz and Oreos and apples we celebrated our own little meal of thanksgiving right then and there.

The approximately 400 mile trip took a little over 22 hours. Twisting, turning switchback roads full of potholes, rocks, and ruts threw us from one side of the "bed" to the other. Slam! Up against the outside wall of the bus you hit if the passenger were on the inside of the bed. Hands clung to the rail so we didn't fall into the aisle for those who were lying on that side. We were banging into each other no matter where we lay as we rocked and rolled through the mountains. At one point during daylight I saw, on the other side of the switchback, a bus on its side, partway down the steep slope of the mountain. It had obviously gone off the road at some point in time and there it remained. Vomit had been the least of those passenger's worries.

I vividly remember praying desperately for the whole thing to be over with. The children did a remarkable job of not complaining or crying—I credit shock and disbelief for that, not to mention terror and fear. I repented of things I'd never done or even thought of doing as I was pretty sure we were on the road to meeting Jesus that day.

Arriving—finally!—in JingHong, we had no idea where to go or where to stay or eat or take care of any other vital human activity. What a horrible, horrible feeling. Somehow we managed to find taxis to take us to the hotel where Ben had made our reservation, and there we showered and enjoyed standing upright with our feet on the solid earth.

Sometimes taking "the road less traveled" leads to adventures that are fun and exciting and wonderful to remember and reminisce about years later, memories that bring joy and laughter and a sense of discovery and awe. Unfortunately, this was not one of those times. Glazed eyes and trembling lips are still the automatic response when the words "Chinese sleeper bus" are mentioned in our family. Maybe the dead guy knew what he was doing after all.

CHAPTER EIGHT

Forgiveness— Giving Before

"*Just* a spoon full of sugar helps the medicine go down." If we were contestants on a quiz show and were asked to name the person who made that statement famous, we'd all be pushing our buzzers to answer. Ah, Mary Poppins, the faultless governess!

As you remember, Mary flew in under her umbrella to serve as nanny for two young children, Jane and Michael Banks, who lived in late 19th-century London. She brought with her a giant, mysterious carpetbag, and among all the surprising goodies she carried in it, one stands out most in my memory: her measuring tape. Not just any measuring tape, this one measured a person's character traits. When she measured Jane and Michael on the day she arrived, Mary obviously wasn't interested in their physical height as she told them, "I want to see how you measure up!"

When she measured Michael, the tape didn't show centimeters. Instead, it read, "Extremely stubborn and suspicious!" And when stretched out from toe to head on Jane, the tape measure read, "Rather inclined to giggle and does not put things away." The children then asked Mary to measure herself, and not surprisingly, the tape at her exact height read, "Mary Poppins. Practically perfect in every way!"

Oh my, oh dear! I will admit that I've had to repent more than once for using a Mary Poppins measuring tape on those around me. In my case, I used my insecurity, fear, and judgment to measure others, and very few people ever quite "measured up" to the standard I had set for them. Of course, *my* standard was surely accurate, as in my own mind it read "practically perfect in every way" when I used it on myself.

The Need to Be Right

Most of us have a deep need to be right. Television quiz shows reward people who answer (or guess) correctly more often than the other contestants. It is important to us that our investments be right, that our theology and political views be, without dispute, right. We want to dress, act, speak, and present ourselves the right way. We invest a lot of time and effort in being *right*.

When we always have to be right…we find ourselves walking a path that leads to many negative consequences in our lives.

When we always have to be right, when we hold a higher standard of judgment for others than we hold for ourselves, we find ourselves walking a path that leads to many negative consequences in our lives. Our perception of situations may actually be correct. We ourselves may be right and other parties involved may indeed be wrong, but in terms of relationships, using a Mary Poppins measuring tape carries a heavy price of brokenness and pain.

The problem is that sometimes our need to be right gets in the way of our dearest relationships and what matters most to us. It can creep in through hurts, unresolved conflicts, pride, insecurity, or not feeling accepted or loved.

Letting Go

Think back on the story about Mrs. Fowler. Which of us, Mrs. Fowler or me, would you choose as being *right* in her behavior? Not Mrs. Fowler! But would it be right for me to hold her in unforgiveness? No! She "done me wrong," but not forgiving her would make no difference to her. I don't even know if she's still alive, and if she is, I doubt that she would remember who I am. My unforgiveness wouldn't hold *her* captive, but would actually keep *me* locked in a place of darkness where a part of me would always remain an orphan, never allowing other people or Papa God to look into my heart. I would still believe the lies that I was stupid and unworthy. There would be no room for the intimacy of knowing that I belong in my heavenly Father's heart because my heart would already be filled with awful pain. It's not easy to forgive people who have wronged us, but it's not easy to carry all the pain that comes when we don't forgive, either. Sometimes our bitterness, anger, resentment, and fear actually cause physical pain. It's as though the pain in our hearts, when not released through forgiveness, leaks out in the form of physical symptoms in our bodies.

Forgiveness Brings Freedom

Unfortunately, the word "forgiveness" has been the subject of some bad PR over the years. We tend to equate forgiving with forgetting, and we fear that if we forgive, injustice will prevail. Somehow we've believed that holding onto unforgiveness is the same thing as serving justice. It is not. For a clearer understanding of biblical forgiveness, let's look at the definition of the word itself.

Somehow we've believed that holding onto unforgiveness is the same thing as serving justice. It is not.

The prefix *for* means ahead, before, or through, and the root *give* means to offer with no expectation of return, to grant or bestow formally, to accord or yield to another. In the context of holding grudges or clinging to wounds inflicted on us by others, putting the prefix and the root together gives us a word that means to go before or ahead of an offense, or perhaps through it, and to give up the claim to requital for it. It denotes the concepts of pardon and of releasing another from payment of debt.

If the word *forgive* makes you defensive or angry, look at it according to the definition. Be first to go ahead and make a present to those who have hurt you. The present you are giving? Your choice is to release your offenders from having to repay you for what they did or took. You might think you're letting them off the hook, but what you're actually doing is removing from your own mind and heart the chains that have kept you tied in knots all these years.

Unforgiveness Stinks!

I don't know if you live in an area where skunks live in the wild, but if you do, you have experienced the offensive, acrid smell they make in self-defense. When you refuse to forgive others, it's as though you have been sprayed by a skunk and refuse to wash it off. If you take an "I'll show him" attitude, who suffers? You, and those around you. The skunk has gone home.

Some of us even pick up the dead skunks of painful memories and put them in our back pockets. We don't want anyone telling us what to do with the skunk that hurt us, and we're determined never to forget the offense. Trust me: with that attitude, you don't forget, no matter how hard you try. Every time you try to rest, you find yourself disturbed by the bump in your back pocket, not to mention the smell. You also become so defensive that no one wants to be around you anymore! Even the people you thought were your friends are nowhere in sight. Perhaps it has something to do with the odor of Pepe LePew in your back pocket. Nobody likes the smell of a skunk!

In reality, those who have hurt us may or may not realize that their words or actions have caused us pain.

You see, forgiveness has been given a bad rap. Too many people see it as giving the offender a free ticket:

Now he'll never have to pay for what he did. Says who? Mary Poppins or Papa God? God is the one who sees and weighs our hearts. When we refuse to forgive, we usually think that we're keeping our offender in prison and that we—the judge and jury—have decided never to let him out! In reality, those who have hurt us may or may not realize that their words or actions have caused us pain. In fact, they may not recall the incident at all, or in some cases, even remember who we are. So who is really in prison? The one who is still holding tight to the pain, unable to believe that getting rid of the skunk carcass is the passkey to freedom.

Think Thoughts of Life

Think about what you're thinking about! All day long your mind is thinking about something. Have you ever stopped to think about what your thoughts are at any given moment? I encourage you to begin doing that, and then ask yourself, "Why am I thinking about this?" You can choose whether to agree with that thought or to reject it. You can embrace it or refuse to entertain it.

We all have difficult people in our lives. I learned through the teaching of Shiloh Place Ministries that we can list most of our thoughts and mental conversations about a person under one of two categories: thoughts of restoration and relationship or thoughts of vindication and exposure. One way leads to blessing, the other to a self-imposed curse. God wants even our difficult relationships to release blessing into our lives.

Sow Forgiveness, Reap Mercy

It isn't just a matter of what we want to give to those who have hurt us; it's a matter of what we want to reap from other relationships in the future. If we sow anger and unforgiveness, we will reap wounded hearts that keep us from intimacy with God. Healthy relationships will be difficult for us to maintain; it's hard to find loyal friends when we smell of dead skunk. If we sow forgiveness and blessing and mercy, we will enjoy a life of peace and joy. Our attitudes will be gentle and accepting toward others, and our stomachs won't be tied up in knots when we see a difficult person or hear his name.

If we sow anger and unforgiveness, we will reap wounded hearts that keep us from intimacy with God.

You see, we give to others what we have received, and we receive from others what we have given. *"Such as I have, give I thee"* (Acts 3:6 KJV). Hebrews 4 tells us that Jesus wants to give us rest. Papa God isn't a slave driver who demands perfection from us, nor does He look at us with disgust when we don't measure up. He is a wonderful, safe, kind, patient Dad who wants us to love Him and to know His embrace. He looks at us with the look of love, and He wants us to rest in the assurance that we belong in His heart.

Look back once again at the hallway scene with Mrs. Fowler. In it, Jesus shows Himself as a protector, saying, "Don't you judge My people!" He did not want my teacher to judge me the way she did, but He didn't want me to judge her either. He has forgiven me for every sin I have ever committed, so how can I hold Mrs. Fowler in the prison of unforgiveness? He's given me the gift of freedom that I didn't deserve. Such as I have, I will give.

I have heard my pastor Bill Johnson say that the law of grace interrupts the law of sowing and reaping. By receiving the grace of God's forgiveness ourselves, we can then extend that grace to others, and as we forgive, more grace and more forgiveness is what we will begin to reap.

On more than one occasion I've had people tell me they don't know how to forgive. Here is a simple, step-by-step walk through the grace of forgiveness:

1. As forgiveness is a gift, picture yourself writing a list of all the things for which you need to forgive your offender.

2. See yourself placing that list which represents your forgiveness in a gift box.

3. Imagine wrapping the box with expensive paper and a lavish bow.

4. Who will you give your gift of forgiveness to? Write their name on the gift tag.

5. You now have a box of forgiveness: what you have, you can give. Picture yourself handing the box to the one you are forgiving.

6. Let go of the box as they receive your offer of grace.

7. Thank the Lord for the freedom you have now that the "skunk" is gone!

Prayer

Will you join me in prayer?

Dear heavenly Father, I come to You in Jesus' name.

I come to say I am so grateful that You love me as I am and not the way others say I should be. Thank You for looking at me in love, even when I didn't know that You were and didn't realize that You are good. I confess that I have not been living life Your way, but instead have been trying on my own to be and do all things right. My pride has prevented the kind of relationship with You and others that I could have had. I have been critical and judgmental of others, and now I understand the high price I've paid for what I've done. I repent of my sins, and I ask You to forgive me and make me clean so that I can have an open, loving, intimate relationship with You.

I choose, Lord, to forgive each person who has hurt me. I confess that I have kept (list them by name and forgive each offense) in a prison that I created in my mind. I forgive those who have misrepresented Your love to me. I release them to be all You want them to be, and I thank You that I am now free to fulfill the purpose for which You created me, as well.

Father, please help me to have a correct view of who I am and to find my worth in You and Your love for me rather than in what I can do for You. I choose to walk in humility, not pride. I choose to value my relationships with others more than my need to be right.

Thank You for the patient love You've shown me. I love You, Papa, and am so thankful to be called Your child.

Amen.

CHAPTER NINE

He's Restoring
Our Soul

Typhoid Fred

Fred had only come south to check on the job because of peer pressure. His best friend Ben had convinced him that the job opportunity in the rain forest was worth moving away from family and adapting to the unfamiliar heat and humidity. So Fred's body came for the interview, but it was obvious that his heart was back home in the cooler north.

A couple of days into the interview process, Fred was still moping around. Jim and I weren't sure how much of his attitude was due to homesickness and how much of it was simply that the interview wasn't his idea to start with, so when he called to say that he was going to the doctor, we gave him a pat reply and didn't think much of it. Doctors couldn't cure homesickness, and Fred was scheduled to go back to his hometown at the end of the week, so we shrugged it off as his emotions getting the better of him.

He called a few hours later to say that he wanted to join us, as his plans had changed, and he'd be traveling home the next day. A number of us were enjoying dinner together in an outdoor café under the shade of banana trees, and we encouraged Fred to come on over. Dishes of vegetables, fish, and dumplings loaded down the lazy

Susan on the tabletop, and we were digging into the community bowls of food.

Fred soon arrived, looking like a whipped pup, his face sad and drawn and his countenance droopy. Seeing that he wasn't hooked up to an IV stand and thinking that the idea of going home should have cheered him up, we assumed that he was fine. We kept joking around amongst ourselves, hoping he'd join in. We made sure that he had a rice bowl, a pair of chopsticks and some green tea, and we encouraged him to dig into the dishes of food we were all sharing.

It became apparent that our idea of drawing him into our shared joy wasn't going to work, so finally I asked Fred what the doctor had said. He told us that he'd been given some medication and had been told that he should start to feel better in a week, but he couldn't remember just what the disease was called in English. Oh yes, he remembered: he'd written it on his hand. Knowing that we would ask, he had wanted to be sure to tell us the right name. He held up his hand, and we saw the diagnosis he'd been given, written with a black felt pen in capital letters: *typhoid*.

**After a deep gasp from
every diner at the table,
the only sound
to be heard was the
click of chopsticks
dropping from our hands.**

After a deep gasp from every diner at the table, the only sound to be heard was the click of chopsticks dropping from our hands. As we considered how many times Fred had dipped his chopsticks into the bowls along with ours, our appetites were suddenly gone.

Inspired by Elijah the prophet, we immediately prayed, "No death in the pot!" (see 2 Kings 4:38-41). The next day we gladly sent Fred home, where he quickly recovered his health and his sense of humor. Although I think it's fair to say that the rest of us had a few anxious moments in the next few days, God heard our Elijah-inspired cry, and not one of us got sick. To this day I admit that when I join Fred for a meal, I am sure to ask how he's been feeling before we dig in.

Be Still, My Soul

Just thinking about being exposed to a communicable disease can cause fear and anxiety! Thankfully, most of us never have to think about it or deal with it, but unfortunately it doesn't take such obvious or dramatic incidents to strike our souls with a blow of anxiety.

Anxiety is "fearful concern, painful or apprehensive uneasiness of mind, an overwhelming sense of apprehension and fear." It stems from the Latin root *anxius,* meaning to strangle or distress.[1]

The soul is made up of mind, will, and emotion, so to be anxious is to have a fearful mind, or an overwhelming emotional sense of apprehension or fear. It is to have our wills—our sense of purpose and determination—strangled or distressed. The effects of stress can be overwhelming. They have been studied endlessly and expounded in volumes of medical and psychological journals. My purpose here is not to define all that fear and anxiety are and all the ways they come to us, but rather to help find a remedy and antidote.

Healing in His Presence

Looking back at "The Fowler's Snare" story, I began to see on another level what Jesus has done to make me whole. You will recall that in the vision He allowed me to see that I was hidden in Him, surrounded and covered by His very presence. What I realized was that when my teacher said those horrible things to me, her words flew out of her mouth with a force of death and hurt intended for my soul, but in reality they never reached me because I was in Christ Jesus.

I began to understand that the impact of those negative words hit Jesus, not me.

I began to understand that the impact of those negative words hit Jesus, not me. He absorbed the pain and insult of them, and I watched in awe as each word hit Him hard enough to produce a bruise. I remembered Isaiah 53:5, which says:

> *But He was wounded for our transgressions, He was bruised for our iniquities; the chastisement for*

*our peace was upon Him, and by His stripes we
are healed* (NKJV).

What a revelation! I know that a bruise is produced
by an impact to the skin and that a bruise heals from the
inside out. I realized that whenever hurtful words or painful deeds are aimed at us, Jesus Himself bears the impact
of them, and He is bruised. Hurtful words and deeds do
come against our souls, but when we are in Him, covered
and protected by His presence, we realize that He has tak-
en the blows for us. In this realization, we begin to heal
from the inside out. When we comprehend that He really
has taken the pain intended for us, in whatever form it
comes, we are healed and our souls are made free.

A Peaceful Soul in Anxious Times

To say that the days we are living in are stressful times
is to put it mildly! We are all aware that social, economic,
and governmental factors are converging to cause anxiety.
The question is: what can we do about it?

Just a few weeks ago, I found myself feeling extremely
uncertain, nervous, and even a bit afraid. As you have read,
I have had many times in my life during which anxiety was
my constant state. I have likewise experienced many times
that the Lord Jesus has come and shown me both His presence in my life and the Father's love for me, thereby healing
my soul. So when anxiety started coming on so strong in
me recently, it really caught me by surprise. Jim and I have
walked through lots of changes this past year, but through
it all I hadn't felt this measure of anxiety.

I tried looking at my past and present circumstances, but I could not figure out why I was feeling this way. It wasn't normal for me, and I didn't like the feelings one little bit. On some days I was almost overwhelmed by sadness and had no idea why.

Because God in His goodness desires to see me set totally free, His agape hasn't stopped pursuing me.

Then a friend gave me a copy of Chuck and Pam Pierce's book, *The Rewards of Simplicity.*[2] As I read Chuck's insights on anxiety, I realized that I was reading about myself. Chuck's description of "living life on high alert" made me think of all the times I had nearly jumped out of my skin when someone unexpectedly walked into the room. I came to see that my muscle tension and my waking up tired had oftentimes been directly related to my anxiety. As I delved into Chuck's excellent teaching on dealing with anxiety, I realized that the Lord had put His finger on a deep level of anxiety in my soul that I had not yet confronted. Like an onion being peeled, layers of fear had been pulled off my life over the years, but there are layers yet to go. Because God in His goodness desires to see me set totally free, His agape hasn't stopped pursuing me.

We live in a time when the earth itself is shaking and quaking. Governments and economies are in turmoil, and many of our young people are growing up in a fatherless society. In the midst of it all, God's call is ringing out loud and clear to remind us that He is good. Much of our fear and confusion have come from forgetting one of the deepest, most profound theological truths: God is good; the devil is bad. In the midst of a rapidly changing world, this is a basic truth we must once again believe and embrace. An example of how confused we've become can be seen by asking ourselves which of these questions in each set is Biblically accurate:

God gave me this sickness to teach me something. Or—God doesn't have sickness so He can't give it. Sickness is of the devil.

God is watching over me to see if I mess up so He can discipline me.

Or—God is watching over me with love.

I messed up. I'm a failure.

Or—I made a mistake but that's not who I am.

As the Agape Reformation spreads throughout the land, much of the confusion we've had concerning God's character is being replaced with truth. As careful as we are not to catch even the common cold from someone else, we must become even more careful not to catch a common belief about our heavenly Father that does not line up with what He says about Himself in His Word. It is time that we, as His children, learn to take every thought captive to make it line up with Truth (see 2 Cor. 10:4-5). In that way we can live peaceful, intentional lives even in the midst of societal change.

Hooked up to an Intravenous Drip of Comfort

We can't change the way we think—repent—about something until we become aware of how we think and recognize a better option. That is what Holy Spirit was doing for me when He showed me the deeper levels of anxiety that I still needed to address. He wasn't pointing them out to show me how lousy and awful I am. Remember, that's neither His heart nor His way. He was showing me the dry and desperate condition of my soul so that I could let go of the wrong ways I was seeing the Father and myself. He was inviting me into the healing presence that is available when we know we belong in our Father's heart.

I'll admit, though, that when I realized I was dealing with anxiety, my first reaction was to feel guilty. Oh yeah, that's a great solution! Add one wrong response to another! So I repented of that, as well, and asked Him to show me in His Word how to deal with it.

The Lord led me to Psalm 94, which describes God as our refuge. Verses 12-13a read,

> *Blessed is the man whom You instruct, O Lord, and teach out of Your law, that You may give him rest from the days of adversity…*

Then, verses 17-19 seemed to shout out to me:

> *Unless the Lord had been my help, my soul would soon have settled in silence. If I say, "My foot slips," Your mercy, O Lord, will hold me up. In*

the multitude of my anxieties within me, Your comforts delight my soul (NKJV).

There it was! Rest and comfort—just what my soul was crying out for and just what He offers every day. I knew I was in good company when the psalmist didn't gloss over or deny his own anxiety but rather admitted it and then praised God for His solution: the rest and comfort we receive from being in Papa's presence, from knowing that we belong in His heart, from knowing that He is looking at us with love.

Therein is our healing. Being connected to the very love of God, walking through life hooked up to an invisible IV drip, being transfused with the hope and peace and joy He and He alone can give.

Drip, drip, drip.

That's My Daddy!

Knowing who our heavenly Father is—knowing His love and delight in us—brings healing and rest to our souls. Yes, we live in a day of great turmoil all over the world. In the natural, these are days of great trial, and men's souls and hearts are failing them for fear (see Luke 21:26 NKJV). But this is also a day when Father God—Papa, Daddy—is revealing Himself in a new way. He is calling us back to His love and His embrace. He is offering us the opportunity to know Him with an intimacy that restores our joy and causes our souls to be like well-watered gardens (see Jer. 31:12).

Knowing who our Heavenly Father is—knowing His love and delight in us—brings healing and rest to our souls.

Allow Him to show you the areas in your life where you are still thinking and acting like an orphan. Ask Him to peel back your layers of fear and anxiety and to bring the healing that comes when the truth of His great love for you drips into the dry parts of your soul.

Prayer

Read this Scripture as a prayer, and as you do, may you experience the reality of His presence right there in the room where you are. Like Miriam of old, may you rejoice and dance and be satisfied with your Father, for He is very, very good.

> *"...They* [God's people] *will come and shout for joy on the heights of Zion; they will rejoice in the bounty of the Lord....They will be like a well-watered garden, and they will sorrow no more. Then young women will dance and be glad, and young men and old as well. I will turn their mourning into gladness; I will give them comfort and joy instead of sorrow. I will satisfy the priests with abundance, and My people will be filled with my bounty," declares the Lord* (Jeremiah 31:12-14).

ENDNOTES

1. Merriam-Webster's Collegiate Dictionary, 11th ed., s.v. "anxiety."

2. Chuck Pierce and Pam Pierce, *The Rewards of Simplicity* (Grand Rapids, MI: Chosen Books, 2010).

CHAPTER TEN

I'm Afraid—Not!

*A*lthough I was just a little girl, not even yet in school, I remember knowing that Becky was wrong and I was right. I mean, it was obvious. As we sat on her front porch with our coloring books and pack of 64 crayons, she told me I wasn't doing it right. Doing it right? How can you color wrong? When I posed a question along that line, she, being a full year wiser, informed me that coloring "wrong" meant that I wasn't staying in the lines. Everyone knew that to color "right" one carefully traced the outline on the page and then colored inside the lines. That nice, heavy outline created the "correct" boundary, apparently, and Becky had the art of coloring inside the lines perfected. I may have been little, but I distinctly remember thinking she was crazy. After all, whose page was more colorful and interesting, hers or mine? Mine, obviously. What was she thinking?

 To be extravagant is fun…
it makes life and coloring
books much more interesting.

You see, even then I was grasping something that children everywhere know until someone "teaches it out of them": to be extravagant is fun. It's colorful. And it makes life and coloring books much more interesting.

The word *extravagant* was crafted to describe displays of beautiful excess that knows no boundaries. The first part of the word, *extra*, of course means more than enough, more than is due, more than usual or necessary. It also conveys a sense of special or superior quality, as in extra-strength mouthwash. The word *extra* lets you know that you have something special in your hand when you buy that one. The second part of the word comes from the Latin root word *vagari*, which means to wander about. Putting the two together, we have the word *extravagant*, which means to exceed the limits and boundaries of reason, to go beyond what is necessary. Profuse. Lavish.[1] It makes me think of coloring outside the lines.

While you may have liked Becky's neat, yellow duck, and though you may have thought her carefully outlined and colored picture sweet, you certainly would have noticed my blue, purple, red, and orange slashes, my squiggles of color, and the black outline of a cow showing through here and there. Extravagance makes you look and wonder.

Time to Resign

Three decades later, I once again found myself coloring outside the lines. I had spent those interim years dedicated to doing what I thought was expected of me by others and God. I was trying so hard to "color inside the lines" of what I thought it meant to be a good Christian. The problem was that in the process I became afraid. The list of my fears was nearly endless, from spiders to the dark to embarrassing myself in social situations. I was married and starting a family, which added to the list of things I could be afraid of. All it took was watching the news to know that divorce was rampant, that children could be in danger just walking to school, and that if food prices kept rising, we'd have to worry about how to feed our little ones. War was discussed far too often, and I had nothing nice enough to wear to the birthday party this weekend.

> **As long as I was willing to entertain them, fears were willing to come for an extended stay, bringing their fellow fears with them.**

You see, none of my fears had to make logical sense or even fit together in the same thought. As long as I was willing to entertain them, fears were willing to come for an extended stay, bringing their fellow fears with them. The problem was that most of what I feared had no basis in the reality of my day-to-day life. It was as though my mind and emotions were out of control, and all I had to do was think of something to fear, agree with the fact that it was scary, and there it was—another fear wrapped around my life.

I don't remember the day or the occasion on which I suddenly decided I'd had enough: enough living in fear, enough bowing my knee to the "what ifs." I realized that I must either resign myself to a life lived in fear or resign from being afraid. Choosing to walk away from anxiety and dread, I began the process of turning back to Jesus and pouring out my heart to Him about all the things I was afraid of. I would tell Him about a fear I was entertaining and ask Him His opinion of it. What a relief, what a burst of freedom to realize that He wasn't afraid of any of those things. And since He had come to live in me, I didn't have to be either.

One by one, I looked at my fears. I would act as though I was putting a particular fear in my hand and then hand it to Him to manage. Admitting I'd been wrong to carry this fear with me, I would ask Jesus to forgive me for trusting the darkness more than I'd trusted Him, the Light of the World, and I asked Him to clean my heart and mind and set me free. In this way, step by step, I walked out of fear and into knowing that, because God is good, I never have to be afraid.

Now and then I found that old feeling of fear coming on me again, and as soon as I recognized what it was, I would say something like this out loud: "satan, thank you for reminding me that Jesus took that fear from me and set me free. I've forgotten to praise Him for that today!" Then I would begin thanking Jesus extravagantly for taking my fears away and giving me courage, for loving me so much that He doesn't want me to be afraid. You know, that's not the reaction those old fears expected, and when I turned their visit into an occasion to praise Jesus, they didn't stop by again. I turned in my resignation from being in fear's employ, and I was now fully committed to becoming as courageous and free in Jesus as possible.

God's Extravagant Expression of Love

When I began to read about all the good Jesus did and His purpose of showing us what the Father is like, the light began to go on inside of me. I saw that Jesus is God's extravagance, displayed for us to see. God could have sent a rigid, stern savior who did everything that the religious community expected of him. He could have sent one who just colored inside the lines all the time and "got the job done." Instead, He sent Jesus, the God-man who colored outside the lines and loved those whom no one else could or would. Jesus, who laughed and cried, held children in His arms, and spoke kindly to women and men alike. He was an extravagant Savior who gave all He had, who didn't stay inside the lines of religious tradition—and His words and actions caused people to look and wonder.

 I saw that Jesus is God's extravagance, displayed for us to see.

I experienced an unexpected benefit of rejecting fear, which was that the Bible began to sound much more positive! Instead of reading it and seeing all the "do nots," I found life and hope in its pages. Instead of feeling the pressure to have enough faith, I now saw that trusting my Lord brings me rest. Instead of "thou shalt not," I began to see that the law pointed out my deep need for Jesus, who fulfilled it.

Now, when fear or anxiety try to take root in my soul, I read the Bible until a passage seems to leap off the page and speak right to me. This Book is alive and speaks to the issues of our hearts today. I especially like to read Psalms and the Book of Isaiah, and I have underlined and dated many passages over the years that have helped me through difficult situations. When I find a Scripture that helps me, I write what is going on and record the date it spoke to me beside the verse, and it becomes a written testimony to remind me of how God has helped me. The next time, even years later, that my eyes are drawn to that passage, reading my own written testimony of His deliverance builds my faith to expect Him to intervene and help once again.

Imagine That!

Our imaginations are powerful and can be used either as weapons against our good or tools to help us prosper. The Bible is often misquoted as stating that we are to suppress our imaginations, as it leads to harm. What it actually says is that we are to cast out of our minds every imagination that wants to be higher in our decision making and consciousness than knowing God (see 2 Cor. 10). We aren't to cast out imagination! Rather, we are to be sure that our imaginations line up with what is noble, pure, lovely, and just (see Phil. 4:8). *Imagination* comes from a root word that means to imitate; we will start to look and act like those things that we observe. When our imaginations are set on trying to know how good God is, or how kind or how happy, then that is the direction our hearts follow.

We are to be sure that our imaginations line up with what is noble, pure, lovely, and just.

Our imaginations are also linked to our expectations. What we imagine is what we expect. I think of the word *expectation* as expecting action. My imagination tells my emotions what action to expect. If I see my Father as good, I expect Him to act in goodness toward me. If I see Him as angry and mean, then I expect anger and meanness from Him. So, when I used to imagine that I would be unhappy or unsuccessful in a given situation, I usually was. My imagination was set on how I would blunder or be afraid, so my expectation was for failure and fear. You can imagine what I got: failure and fear. I expected God to be disappointed in me, so no matter how hard I tried or how well I did, my imagination told me it wasn't good enough to please Him.

As I began to realize that God has goodness and peace and favor in store for me, I could begin to imagine that situations would work out well. I went into them with an expectation of seeing Him help me and protect me. Guess what I started getting? Peace and joy and courage. I know He loves me enough to bring correction to me when I mess up, but He brings it in love and gentleness. I expect my good Papa to be good to me, and that takes away any room for fear and terror.

He's Better Than You
Imagine Him to Be!

We live in a time where there is much to fear, naturally speaking. Not only are nations changing and warring, but even the earth itself is shaking and quaking and blowing off steam. There isn't a lot of good news on television, and some days it seems as though a sense of dread and anxiety about what will happen next passes through the very airwaves.

Over and over in the Bible, people are admonished, "Do not be afraid!" Most of the time they are told this because in the natural there's plenty of reason for fear! But into that fearful situation the word is given, "Don't be afraid." Just as Peter and John at the Gate Beautiful could only give what they had, Papa God can only give to us what He has. And He doesn't have fear. He doesn't have lack. He doesn't have anxiety. Our Father is Love. Jesus is Peace. Holy Spirit is the Comforter. That's what He offers to us.

However good you perceive God to be, He's better than that. However completely you think He loves, He loves much more than that. However large you think the parameters of His willingness to forgive you and accept you back fully into His embrace, the lines and parameters are bigger than that. Besides, He's an extravagant God. He has colored outside every line imaginable to show you how huge and alive, how colorful and welcoming is His invitation to trust Him in the times of your greatest fear. That's why He said in Psalm 37, *"Fret not, it only leads to harm"* (NKJV).

However good you perceive God to be— He's better than that.

Whatever the situations that have caused you to live in fear, you can repent of them and hand them over to the Prince of Peace. To repent is to admit your fear, hand it to Him, and ask Him to forgive you. Then, remembering that you belong in His heart, begin thanking Him for being so extravagant in His love that He has gone before you to walk with you and protect you from behind.

Go ahead: color outside the lines! Let your faith rise so that others will see how you trust your Father to take care of you. Peace and joy will spill out of you as you expect His actions on your behalf to be full of love and protection and grace. May your life be such an expression of His goodness that it causes others to look and wonder!

Prayer

Dear Good Father,

How grateful I am that You are Light and that there is no darkness in You! I confess I have been afraid many times and have allowed fear to steer my imagination away from You. Please forgive me, make me clean, and help me recapture the feeling of safety and protection that I had the day I first met You. I know that fear lives in and is empowered by darkness, so I choose today to give You all my fears, to resign from giving them power over my life, and to step back into the Light that is found in Your presence. I remember once again whose I am, and the reminder of how You love me makes all my fear leave. What an honor to be Your adopted child, Papa! I set my heart to begin imagining how good and kind You are, and my expectations line up with what the Word of God says about how You consider me.

Thanks, too, for all the colors of the rainbow with which to express my love for You! I'm going to follow Your lead and color outside the lines of the box I tried to keep You in. I want my life to express Your heart so boldly that I become a sign and a wonder that points others to Your Light.

I love You, Lord!

Amen.

ENDNOTE

1. Merriam-Webster's Collegiate Dictionary, 11th ed., s.v. "extravagant."

Postscript

I thought I was finished writing with the previous chapter, but there is yet a story begging to be told. As you read this story of a father's love, I ask that you read it with eyes of hope for yourself or someone you love. Please look at what happened and realize the greater story behind it and the deeper love you are being invited into.

Jim and I minister in numerous nations as well as many cities in the United States. We have seen the devastation in lives wrecked by fatherlessness. We have heard the stories, shared through gut-wrenching tears, of young girls rescued out of prostitution. We have held in our arms young women rescued from the horrors of child soldier camps. And we have wept with young ladies who were afraid to go home, knowing what awaited them there when the darkness of night fell. We are not unaware of the pain of sin, both that chosen willingly and that forced upon us by another's sick desire.

So I do understand that not everyone reading this can relate to a loving, good, safe father. But I also have seen and know the healing and freedom that is available to each one of us when we come to understand that Father God is good and loves us. I am blessed to have had a great dad, but not because I deserved it. My dad is not perfect or nearly as good as God, and neither is my husband! And neither of them would ever want me to portray to you that they are. Yet both are godly, good men whose lives show me an example of who Papa God is. The example they have shown me I now share with you. May it help seal in your heart how deeply loved you are and always have been.

I don't understand why some things happen as they do, but I do know that our good Papa God loves it when we share the testimony (story) of what He has done for us and throw it out as a lifeline to those still sinking in father-lessness and longing to belong. As you read this story of my dad and me, the question is not, "What is wrong with me that I didn't have that kind of dad?" Rather, the question is: Will you accept the invitation Papa is extending to you as you read it to climb up out of your pain and into the safety of belonging in His heart? He's waited all day to just spend time together with you.

EPILOGUE

Waiting for Him to Come

*I*t was almost time for Daddy to come home from work, and I was ready. At just four years old, I couldn't yet tell time, but I didn't need a clock to tell me that he would soon be home. It seemed that there was a skip in my step that had been missing all day as, holding tight to my Snow White book, I paced back and forth from living room to dining room in anticipation. When I heard the crunch of his mail truck on our red dog road and the slam of his truck door shutting behind him, it was as if my day got a fresh new start.

Of all the emotions in my childhood, fear is the one I remember most, especially as a little girl, probably because so many things had happened in my young life that I had no way of comprehending. While I may have been safe at all times and not realized it because of the trauma of my mother's death, I remember being afraid all day, every day.

That is, until it was time for my Dad to come home. Every day I was filled with the same gleeful anticipation of having my daddy home, and just seeing him walk in the door reassured me that all was right with my world.

I can still see it as clearly as though it happened yesterday instead of decades ago. Every day, having finished delivering the mail on his appointed rounds, Daddy walked in the door to the dining room, set his lunch box on the table, smiled at me, and kissed my stepmom. After a quick drink of iced tea from the fridge, he and I were off to the living room and his big recliner chair, where he read the adventures of Snow White to me once again. I remember one day when my stepmom asked me a reasonable question: "Don't you think your dad would like to read something else for a change?"

I also remember his amazing response: "If Brenda wants me to read her this book every day for the rest of her life, I will gladly do it!"

He allowed me to linger there as long as I needed and until I was ready to go.

When Dad reclined his overstuffed chair and opened the book, I carried out a plan of my own. I didn't listen to the story; I'd already heard it so many times that I could quote the pages by heart. Instead, I used my ears to listen for my dad's heartbeat. Pressing my right ear as close to his chest as possible, I slowed down or sped up my own breathing, trying to get my heart to beat with the same rhythm as his. I remember that on some days he finished the story and was ready to do something else before I had achieved my goal, and I would tell him, "No! Not yet, Dad!" Whether he realized what I was doing or not, I have no idea. What I do know is that he never shooed me away. He allowed me to linger there as long as I needed and until I was ready to go.

And when to the best of my ability our hearts were beating as one, I jumped down off Daddy's lap, my fears now replaced by a deep sense of safety and peace. I could face whatever came my way for the rest of the evening. My father and I had the same heartbeat. I was at home in his love, and that's where I belonged.

The Party Has Begun!

Recklessly Extravagant

*T*here it is! I found it again, the absolute extravagance of God. And you'll never believe where it's been hidden all these years? In the story of what we call "The Prodigal Son" (see Luke 15).

I remember back to when I was 15 years old and in youth group. The word *prodigal* bothered me because I didn't know what it meant, and I didn't like not knowing words and their meanings. Recently I was reminded of the definition I learned all those years ago.

If you look up the word *prodigal* in Merriam-Webster's dictionary (Collegiate, Tenth Edition) you'll see that the first definition given for the word *prodigal* is "recklessly extravagant." We've already determined that to be extravagant is to go beyond the limits and boundaries of reason. To color outside of the lines, if you will.

In this parable, found in Luke 15:11-32, Jesus told the story of a father who had two sons. The younger son demanded his inheritance from his father, and the father divided his estate between the two boys. The younger son went off into the world and wasted what he had been given. Jesus did not call the son "prodigal," but in some versions of the Bible his wasteful way of living is translated "prodigal living" (NKJV). He was definitely reckless and extravagant in the ways he spent his inheritance. He ended up so destitute that he took a job for a hog farmer, even eating the slop that he was feeding the pigs. The Word tells us that one day he came to himself and decided to go home. He would repent to his father and ask to be taken in as a servant.

Meanwhile back at the ranch we are told that the older son was being such a good boy! He worked hard and never gave his father any reason for pain or alarm. He was trying to be as good as he could, perhaps hoping to never make his father sad again, having seen his despair when the younger son left home. This older son was extravagant in his work ethic, dotting every "i" and crossing every "t" where the family farm was concerned.

What about the father? I find it interesting that all that we know about him is that he was watching and waiting for the younger son to come home. We know that because we are told in verse 20 "*And he* [the younger son] *arose and come to his father. But **when he was still a great way off**, his father saw him and had compassion, and ran and fell* *on his neck and kissed him*" (NKJV). This son hadn't tex-ted his dad to tell him he was coming, nor had he posted on Facebook that he was repentant and coming home, so the father had no prior warning that the son was coming home this particular day. This tells me the dad was watch-ing every day, looking down the road, anticipating the day his son would return home where he belonged. And then when he got home, still smelling of pig (such an offense to the religious standard of the Jewish law!), the father saw him, ran to him, hugged and kissed him. He gave him his best robe (to identify that he belonged to him), put a ring on his hand (to signify restored authority in the fam-ily), and put sandals on his feet (to represent a new way of walking from now on). Then he proclaimed a celebra-tion, and a party was thrown in the son's honor. A calf was butchered and steaks thrown on the barbeque! Talk about "reckless extravagance!" This father held nothing back.

It is interesting that the older son, who owned the entire farm, became angry when he heard the sound of music and dancing and realized it was in celebration of his brother's return. He was offended that no party had ever been held for him: he had never been feted with a barbeque!

I love the father's response when he says to the older brother, "You've always been right here with me. You *own* the calves on the farm! It's all been yours all along to enjoy. Don't you get it? Your brother was lost and now he is found. He was dead and now he's alive again. Son, relax and enjoy the party!" (Luke 15:31-32, author's paraphrase!)

Is anyone else convicted by the realization that the elder son had been working so hard for the father, doing all the right things, that he never even entertained the thought of a party? There was so much work to be done and no time for celebration! The wrong, sad conviction that was true only in the elder brother's mind has sadly also been true in my mind more times than I'd like to admit.

When Jesus told this parable His opening line was: *"A certain man had two sons."* The man was the subject of the sentence. While each character in the story is important in understanding what Jesus was conveying, I believe He wanted us to see the recklessly extravagant love of the father to both of his sons. The son who played by all the rules and the one who went astray were both celebrated and loved by the father.

A World of Peters and Dorothys

The power of stories is that they enable us to see truths embedded in the lives of others. What I see is that we are living in a time when many lives parallel those of two famous story characters, the orphans Peter Pan and Dorothy of *Wizard of Oz* fame.

You will remember that Peter was an orphan who ran away in an effort to never have to grow up and face all that growing up would entail. This tenderhearted young man just couldn't deal with what it would cost him to change enough to fit into society as he saw it. As the story goes, when he was a grown man he recaptured his "happy thought,"—that which kept him going and gave him hope for the future during his growing-up years. The youthful happy thought of this orphan? To be a daddy. While he never felt he fit in the world around him, his one desire above all else was to be a father. To be part of a family.

Dorothy grew up in what appears to be a stable, secure home on a Kansas farm. She was an orphan, being raised by her Uncle Henry and Aunt Em. Though dearly loved by them, Dorothy suspected the grass was greener on the other side of the fence and longed to find her dreams over the proverbial rainbow, far from the simple, safe life she knew. So she ran away and ended up going through all sorts of adventures as she made her way to Oz. The whole point of her journey to Oz was to find the father-figure of Oz, the wizard, who would help her get back home to Kansas. Upon finding him she realized that, unlike her own honest and good uncle and aunt back home on the farm, this wizard was an imposter who demanded far more of her than she was able to give. No matter what she did it would never be enough to satisfy the Wizard of Oz, and Dorothy came to the realization that what she had left in Kansas was what she wanted all along—a good family where she belonged. While the wizard was able to trick Dorothy's friends by giving them token gifts to satisfy their needs for intelligence, courage, and a heart, he was unable to fake meeting the deep need in Dorothy—that of going home. There is nothing else that will ever fit that place of longing in Dorothy—or in any one of us for that matter.

Do you see the correlation between these two story characters and many people in our world today? How many, many people have "tried Jesus" but could never change enough to belong and just gave up trying? How many ran away from what they thought was oppressive and irrelevant to their dreams only to find out they'd been duped into trying to do enough for a "wizard" they could never satisfy? How many gave up on growing up yet deeply long for a father?

The Grapes of His Delight

Harvest time is here. As word gets out that God is good and is watching for His children to come home, you can be sure there are many who will come to their senses, awaken out of their poppy field of dreams and realize they are far from home. With repentant hearts they will head for home, hoping just to find a place somewhere in the back where they can sit, a place to serve and be a servant.

The challenge that lies ahead is not only for those coming home but those who are waiting there for them. In Matthew 20 Jesus told the story of a man who owned a vineyard. It was harvest time and he needed help bringing in the grapes. He hired some workers who started early in the morning working the vines. Realizing the harvest was too large for this many people to bring in, he went out and hired more laborers as the day went on, even up until just before quitting time.

When the day was over, the hired hands lined up for their pay, and you can imagine the shock and disbelief of those who had worked all day in the hot sun when their pay was the same as those who had started work close to the end of the day! They were indignant and complained to the landowner that it wasn't fair. His response was that they had agreed to a certain wage for a day's work, and it was his business if he wanted to pay each one the same. It was his money and his vineyard to do with as he pleased.

Hidden in this parable is a challenge to any of us who, like the older brother in the "prodigal" son story, have been working hard for the Lord for years. Those of us who have done our best to "do it all right" and keep the light on for our family members not yet home will have the challenge of accepting what Papa God does when the "prodigals" begin coming home. Will we respond with pouting as the older brother did when suddenly this "newcomer to the vineyard" is asked to teach instead of us? To lead worship? To head up intercession? Or will we rejoice and celebrate the lost coming back into relationship with the Father and His family, the Church?

Does anyone else remember church in the 1970s? Being from Pennsylvania I was a long way from the Jesus movement that was happening on the West Coast. What I do remember is the church struggling through issues such as women wearing pantsuits instead of skirts to church. Scandalous! Young men with long hair, wearing flip-flops attending service? We'd rather not. Guitars in the sanctuary? What's this world coming to?! You see, it isn't just in Bible stories told in days gone by that the challenge of prodigals coming home has had to be faced. For some of us it has been in our own lifetimes. Lord, for the sake of the Kingdom, help us respond with Your love and compassion this time around!

Hearing Papa's Heart

I realize that in writing this book I have used the word *belong* almost as a cadence throughout. My use of this word was not a matter of oversight on my part, nor the inability to access another word. Rather, I hear it as the heartbeat of Father God to an orphaned, fatherless world. The rhythm coming from His heart, if we slow our breathing down long enough to hear it, is the sure and steady pulse of a Papa longing to hold His children close; for them to know who He is. Can you hear His heart beat? "You belong. You belong. You belong."

How many of us have walked out of families, churches, marriages, or relationships because we "never did belong there?" The Agape Reformation is in full swing and you are invited to join in the party! I can almost smell the charcoal heating up on the barbeque as the band warms up for the celebration of your return. It's OK! You're safe here. There's a robe of identity and a ring of authority that are yours. Put on your dancing sandals, let go of your fear and intimidation, and sing! Dance! Worship as Miriam did, filled with the wonder of a Papa who loves you fully.

Welcome home.

ABOUT
BRENDA VANWINKLE

Brenda and her husband Jim have been in ministry for more than 20 years. Brenda draws from her life experiences of being a pastor's wife, a missionary who has traveled and ministered in numerous countries, and a mother of four grown children.

blueDoor is a Christian women's movement designed to train and equip women to walk in victory. Born out of a desire to see women set free from bondages of all kinds, blueDoor has been shared both in the United States and overseas, reaching women from all walks of life. Its practical, Bible-based teachings help us advance as we let go of the things that hold us back and grab hold of what it means to belong in Father God's heart.

blueDoor is also involved in helping to provide hope to women and children being rescued out of human trafficking and the sex trade.

For more information or to schedule a speaking engagement, you can contact Brenda at:

Website: www.BrendaVanWinkle.com
Mailing address: PO Box 494624,
Redding, CA 96049
Email: blueDoor@brendavanwinkle.com

In the right hands, This Book will Change Lives!

Most of the people who need this message will not be looking for this book. To change their lives, you need to put a copy of this book in their hands.

> But others (seeds) fell into good ground, and brought forth fruit, some a hundred-fold, some sixty-fold, some thirty-fold (Matthew 13:8).

Our ministry is constantly seeking methods to find the good ground, the people who need this anointed message to change their lives. Will you help us reach these people?

> Remember this—a farmer who plants only a few seeds will get a small crop. But the one who plants generously will get a generous crop (2 Corinthians 9:6).

EXTEND THIS MINISTRY BY SOWING 3 BOOKS, 5 BOOKS, 10 BOOKS, OR MORE TODAY, AND BECOME A LIFE CHANGER!

Thank you,

Don Nori Sr., Founder
Destiny Image
Since 1982